THE
WONDER
of the
WORD

THE KINGDOM PASTOR'S LIBRARY

THE WONDER
of the
WORD

Hearing the Voice of God in Scripture

TONY EVANS

MOODY PUBLISHERS

CHICAGO

Portions of this book are adapted from *What Matters Most: Four Absolute Necessities in Following Christ* (Chicago: Moody, 2002) and *The Transforming Word: Discovering the Power and Provision of the Bible* (Chicago: Moody, 2006) by Tony Evans.

Part of the introduction has been adapted from *The Kingdom Agenda: Life Under God* (Chicago: Moody Publishers, 2013).

Unless otherwise noted, Scripture quotations marked NASB are taken from the New American Standard Bible®, copyright © 1960, 1962, 1963, 1968, 1971, 1972, 1973, 1975, 1977, 1995 by The Lockman Foundation. Used by permission. (www.Lockman.org)

Scripture quotations marked ESV are from The Holy Bible, English Standard Version® (ESV®), copyright © 2001 by Crossway, a publishing ministry of Good News Publishers. Used by permission. All rights reserved.

Scripture quotations marked KJV are taken from the King James Version.

Scripture quotations marked NIV are taken from the Holy Bible, New International Version®, NIV®. Copyright © 1973, 1978, 1984, 2011 by Biblica, Inc.™ Used by permission of Zondervan. All rights reserved worldwide. www.zondervan.com. The "NIV" and "New International Version" are trademarks registered in the United States Patent and Trademark Office by Biblica, Inc.™

Edited by Kevin P. Emmert and Michelle Sincock
Interior Design: Erik M. Peterson
Cover Design: Thinkpen Design
Cover photo of open Bible copyright © 2018 by Rawpixel.com/Shutterstock (1061269247). All rights reserved.

Library of Congress Cataloging-in-Publication Data

Names: Evans, Tony, 1949- author.
Title: The wonder of the Word : hearing the voice of God in scripture / Tony Evans.
Description: Chicago : Moody Publishers, 2019. | Series: Kingdom pastor's library | Includes bibliographical references.
Identifiers: LCCN 2018050879 (print) | LCCN 2019004519 (ebook) | ISBN 9780802496904 (ebook) | ISBN 9780802418319
Subjects: LCSH: Bible--Introductions.
Classification: LCC BS475.3 (ebook) | LCC BS475.3 .E93 2019 (print) | DDC 220.6/1--dc23
LC record available at https://lccn.loc.gov/2018050879

All websites and phone numbers listed herein are accurate at the time of publication but may change in the future or cease to exist. The listing of website references and resources does not imply publisher endorsement of the site's entire contents. Groups and organizations are listed for informational purposes, and listing does not imply publisher endorsement of their activities.

We hope you enjoy this book from Moody Publishers. Our goal is to provide high-quality, thought-provoking books and products that connect truth to your real needs and challenges. For more information on other books and products written and produced from a biblical perspective, go to www.moodypublishers.com or write to:

Moody Publishers
820 N. LaSalle Boulevard
Chicago, IL 60610

3 5 7 9 10 8 6 4 2

Printed in the United States of America

All Scripture is inspired by God and profitable
for teaching, for reproof, for correction,
for training in righteousness.

2 TIMOTHY 3:16

◆

Therefore, putting aside all filthiness
and all that remains of wickedness,
in humility receive the word implanted,
which is able to save your souls.

JAMES 1:21

CONTENTS

Introduction 9

1. Authority 13

2. Sufficiency 43

3. Canonicity 63

4. Transmission 81

5. Reception 97

6. Application 111

Appendix A: Recommended Resources 135

Appendix B: Ministry Overview 143

Acknowledgments 151

INTRODUCTION

———————— ◆ ————————

The philosophy on which I base my preaching, teaching, and ministry rests on a simple yet profound biblical worldview: the glory of God through the advancement of His kingdom. This worldview is the unifying theme of Scripture, from the beginning of Genesis to the end of Revelation. The concept of God's kingdom is what ties the entire Bible together. When this central point of connectivity is lost to the reader, it is easy for Scripture to seem like a series of stories, events, and personalities that do not strategically and thematically connect to one another.

The word *kingdom* refers to a realm under the rule of a sovereign. When linked to God, *kingdom* refers to the rule of God in both heaven and earth, encompassing both eternity and time. God's kingdom, therefore, is comprehensive in nature. This kingdom is composed of a ruler (God), rulees (angels and mankind), a realm (all of creation), and regulations (laws).

The Bible unfolds how God's kingdom affects the affairs of men and how God has been, is, and will be receiving glory through His kingdom rule, even when that rule is being opposed by both angels and human beings. While God's kingdom rule takes various forms with varying laws through varying administrations (that is, dispensations), it nonetheless maintains its central goal of bringing God glory, whether through blessing or judgment. The kingdom agenda, then, is the visible manifestation of the comprehensive rule of God over every area of life.

God's kingdom agenda is carried out through four covenantal spheres: the individual, the family, the church, and the government (that is, nations). A *covenant* is a divinely created bond through which God administrates His kingdom program. It establishes a legal relationship in the spiritual realm that is to be lived out in the physical realm. To operate under God's kingdom covenants and their accompanying guidelines is to experience God's greatest involvement and positive engagement within that specific sphere. Conversely, to operate outside of and in opposition to God's kingdom covenants is to experience the negative consequences of not being covenantly covered.

This book on the wonder of God's Word is designed to reflect this kingdom perspective. My goal is that this work will serve as a valuable study resource for serious students of the Bible in order to help them develop a relevant kingdom mindset.

While nothing can be added to or subtracted from God's inerrant Word, I sincerely hope that this book will help you grow in your understanding and application of God's Word (see *The Tony Evans Study Bible* or the *Tony Evans Bible Commentary* for study notes, articles, and supporting materials). Most importantly, I pray that your reading of and studying of the written Word—and obedience to it—will lead you to a deeper, more intimate relationship with the living Word, which will then be manifested in your ministry.

CHAPTER ONE

AUTHORITY

Your role as a pastor rests on the firm foundation of God's Word. How well you understand and apply the principles in God's Word will largely impact how well your congregants understand and apply them. As a pastor, you have been called to exegete Scripture in such a way that others will come to know it and its divine Author more fully. Scripture is living, active, and able to transform lives like no other written work in all of history.

Your role is to declare the application of biblical truth acquired through the study of a passage in its context. And when you publicly interpret and apply God's Word, the Holy Spirit confronts your hearers and brings those who respond into conformity to God's Word. A pastor or church leader who does not passionately love the Word of God, understand its power, and properly exegete and apply its truths should not preach at all. Without an authentic connection to and communication of its precepts and authority, one's sermons will be nothing more than eloquent discourses lacking the authority to transform. Sure, depending on how well you fashion your words or delivery, you may hear an "amen" and receive thanks from your congregants. But last I checked, the goal of pastoring or preaching is not applause.

No. The one main goal of pastoring and preaching is life change. And, lest we succumb to pride over the high calling to shepherd a flock, we need to be reminded that life change can be accomplished only by God Himself. One of the tools God gives us as pastors and leaders to encourage life change is His Word. Isaiah 55:10–11 reminds us of the transformative work of the Word:

> For as the rain and the snow come down from heaven,
> And do not return there without watering the earth
> And making it bear and sprout,
> And furnishing seed to the sower and bread to the eater;
> So will My word be which goes forth from My mouth;
> It will not return to Me empty,
> Without accomplishing what I desire,
> And without succeeding in the matter for which I sent it.

You will never find an unconditional guarantee like this in any other piece of writing—especially one that is still good nearly 3,000 years after it was first made. In fact, you will never find another book that can compete with the Bible in any form or fashion whatsoever. Scripture is the living, active foundation upon which our faith rests.

THE VALIDITY OF GOD'S WORD

Everything we are going to talk about in this book hinges on the fact that the Bible came from God. Scripture is unique because it is not the word of man. It is the Word of God. Now, some people will challenge this claim because they say their book is the Word of God. Mormons make that claim for the Book of Mormon, Muslims make a similar claim for the Qur'an, and cults say the same about their founders' writings.

The problem is that anyone can step forward and claim that he or she has received a revelation from God. So how do we know which claim to believe? Thankfully, we don't have to guess, because there are stringent tests that any writing must pass to be validated as the true Word of God (we will look at some here but also some in chapter 3). Since the Bible claims to be the unique revelation of God, its words must stand out from all other words. It must be self-authenticating.

The most important proof of the Bible's uniqueness is Jesus' testimony to the Scriptures. The main reason we know the Bible is God's Word is that Jesus said so. He used the word *Scriptures* on a number of occasions to describe the Old Testament writings, whether the Law or the prophets (see, for example, Matt. 21:42; 22:29; 26:56). Jesus also made a statement in the Sermon on the Mount that no one can ignore: "Truly I say to you, until heaven and earth pass away, not the smallest letter or stroke shall pass from the Law until all is accomplished" (Matt. 5:18).

One implication of Jesus' statement is that to reject the Bible is to reject Jesus and consider Him a liar. Many people who want to claim Jesus don't want to accept the Bible as His Word. But Jesus ruled out that option when He tied His life and ministry completely to the fulfillment of Scripture. Jesus used the strongest language possible to declare that the Bible is God's Word.

The Bible is also unique in the way it has come to us. The Bible's unity of message is nothing short of a miracle, given that it was written over a period of about fifteen hundred years by forty or more people who lived in several different countries with different cultures and came from various backgrounds.

Just try bringing together a liberator and national leader (Moses), a military general (Joshua), two kings (David and Solomon), a shepherd (Amos), a tax collector (Matthew), some fishermen (Peter and John), and a rabbi (Paul), have them write down even the simplest message, and see if they can agree with each other. That wouldn't happen even if they were in the same room at the same time working with the same set of facts, let alone separated by hundreds of years.

The thin red line of our Redeemer and His blood runs all the way through the Bible—from the first prophecy of a Savior and God's slaying of animals to cover Adam and Eve (Gen. 3:15, 21) to the last chapter of Revelation that invites the redeemed to spend eternity with God (Rev. 22:17). The Bible's message is consistent and unified from beginning to end. The psalmist summarized this in the statement: "The sum of Your word is truth" (Ps. 119:160).

No one but God could make sixty-six books into one perfectly unified document. The unity of the Bible is like that of the human body, in which every part and function can be explained only in reference to the whole (see Ps. 119:160a).

Now someone might say, "You're just using circular reasoning here. You're going to the Bible to authenticate the Bible." Okay, let's use standards for historical literature to help verify its truth and corroborate the Bible's witness to itself.

When I make the argument that history testifies to the veracity of Scripture, I am not talking about the Bible as a supernatural document but as a work of historical literature. The point here is that if people accepted the same standards of validity for the Bible that they readily accept for other historical documents, they would have to admit that the Bible is the most widely attested book ever written.

We can take any figure from history who is no longer on the scene. How do we know that George Washington was our nation's first president? Nobody alive today can say, "I have seen George Washington. I've met him and heard him speak, and I know he was real." We accept the historicity of George Washington because we trust the historical record we have about him. And the same can be said for many other people we could name from history.

One test of the validity of any historical record is its proximity to the life of the person whose history it records. One reason the history of George Washington is considered reliable is that much of it was written during his lifetime by people who saw and knew him, and more of it was written in the years shortly after his death. The closer the historical record is to the person's life, the more valid it becomes.

Well, the Bible comes through with shining colors on this score. The very latest part of the New Testament, the book of Revelation, was written in the 90s AD, about sixty years after Jesus' death. But it was also written by the apostle John, an eyewitness to Jesus' life. That gives his writings added weight.

This is amazing testimony to the Bible's trustworthiness. By comparison, some of the famous writings of antiquity, such as those that tell of people like Julius Caesar, were recorded hundreds of years after the events they describe. Many critics attack the early dates for various books of the New Testament because they know that if they admit that the

Gospels and Epistles were written so soon after Jesus' life and death—mostly by eyewitnesses, their case against the Bible is greatly weakened.

Another test of the Bible's historical validity is the number of existing manuscripts that affirm it. We are told that ten copies exist of the account of Julius Caesar crossing the Rubicon, one of the most famous events of ancient history. The earliest of these manuscripts was written hundreds of years after the event, yet the fact of Caesar's crossing has never been seriously questioned by historians.

But the Bible puts that record, and almost any other historical record, to shame. We have over five thousand copies of the Greek New Testament in existence, from fragments of a single verse to entire books. These copies agree on the basic doctrines of the faith and the important facts of Jesus' life, although there are numerous differences of words and the order of events. This record is unheard of in historical circles.

In addition, only the Bible teaches history in advance. Teaching history in advance sounds like an oxymoron—and it would be for any book but the Bible. God's Word teaches about history hundreds of years before it happens, which is called prophecy. If we had no other validation of Scripture but its fulfilled prophecies, we would still be on very solid ground.

There have been many so-called prophets in history, and some of them seemed to make some accurate prophecies. But the Bible's standard is one hundred percent accuracy, whether the prophecy is one hundred or five hundred years in advance of its fulfillment. It's not even worth discussing other prophets' records, because no prophet in any holy book has ever claimed to prophesy the future on the scale that the Bible does.

One of the Bible's most amazing prophecies to me is one of its most familiar: the prophecy that Jesus Christ would be born in the village of Bethlehem. This prophecy was given in Micah 5:2, which was written about seven hundred years before Christ's birth. Its fulfillment is recorded in Matthew 2:5–6. The time frame of this alone is miraculous, but it's even more so when you consider that Bethlehem is just a dot on the map. In other words, the chances of prophesying Jesus' birth and getting it right by accident are next to none.

And don't forget that biblical prophecy isn't limited to religious events. The book of Daniel contains the progression of the Gentile world powers in the centuries before Christ, written hundreds of years before Alexander the Great and the Greeks defeated the Medo-Persian Empire and then were in turn defeated by the Romans. You can close your Bible and open your history book, and you'll find that God tells the story of world history in advance—because the Bible is prophetic in its teaching. In fact, the prophetic nature of the Bible reaches beyond what is commonly understood as prophecy (or foretelling) of events.

Peter writes that "no prophecy was ever made by an act of human will, but men *moved* by the Holy Spirit spoke from God" (2 Peter 1:21, emphasis added). The Old Testament prophets, like Elijah, Isaiah, and Daniel, were messengers sent by God to carry His words and speak them directly to His people. And while these prophets fall within Peter's intended meaning, a closer look at the biblical use of the term "prophecy" in this verse can help build the case that Peter is using the term to denote all of God's Word. The literal translation of the word "prophecy" comes from the Greek word *propheteia*, which means "speaking forth." Thus, Peter contrasts the possibility of all Scripture being a matter of human action or interpretation with the notice that these prophets were "moved by the Holy Spirit" (2 Peter 1:21).

The Bible is unique not only in its prophecy and Holy Spirit-inspired writings, but also in its preservation. It has survived for several thousand years, even though kings and the world's mightiest powers and intellects have been trying to destroy it for centuries.

Think about it. How many books have not only survived for several thousand years, but also are still being read, debated, and sold around the world today at the level that the Bible is? And Bible societies tell us that when they go into a country where Bibles are scarce, people stand in line for hours and even days to receive a copy.

No book in history has been preserved like the Bible. Why wouldn't it be, if God is the author? He is going to take care of His Book. Nations have outlawed the Bible, tried to destroy every copy, and killed people for translating and printing it. People like William Tyndale and John Wycliffe are among the heroes of the faith who dedicated their lives to making sure we have the Bible in our hands.

The Bible records an amazing story in Jeremiah 36, an attempt made by King Jehoiakim of Judah to destroy God's message that the prophet Jeremiah had recorded on a scroll. The king cut up the scroll and burned it (vv. 22–23), but God simply told Jeremiah to get another scroll and write His Word on it again.

The eighteenth-century French philosopher Voltaire despised the Christian church and boasted that within fifty years of his death, Christianity would be extinct and people would have to go to a museum to see a Bible. Yet after Voltaire died, his house was acquired by the French Bible Society and used to print and distribute Bibles.[1]

God says His Word will stand forever (see Ps. 119:89; Isa. 40:8). "Heaven and earth will pass away, but My words will not pass away," Jesus declared (Matt. 24:35). There is no destroying the Bible, because it is the eternal Word of God.

---

1. Cecil Willis, "The Indestructibility of the Bible," *Truth Magazine* 19, no. 31 (June 12, 1975): 483–85, http://www.truthmagazine.com/archives/volume19/TM019211.html.

THE TRUTH OF GOD'S WORD

What if a college professor stood up before his class one day and said, "I want to begin this philosophy class by getting to the bottom line with a statement that will govern everything we study and talk about this semester. The bottom line of this philosophy class is that there are no absolutes. There is no such thing as absolute truth, no propositions that are true in every circumstance. Let me say it again. The bottom line of this philosophy class is that there are no absolutes."

A student in the back raised his hand and said, "Professor, may I ask a question?"

"Yes."

"You said there is no such thing as absolutes, and no such thing as a statement of absolute truth. Are you absolutely sure about that? Because if you are, you have just given us a statement of an absolute that is true in every circumstance, which is a contradiction of the assertion you just made that there are no absolutes."

That exchange may sound like the kind of academic double-talk that makes parents wonder what their children are learning in college and why they have to pay so much for it. But the student who challenged his professor made a very important and valid point about the issue of truth, and about the absurdity in denying the existence of a concept called truth.

How would you react to a doctor who was unsure of

his diagnosis of your condition, but gave you a prescription anyway, which you took to a pharmacist who wasn't even sure he was giving you the medicine the doctor had hesitantly prescribed? You would probably run from both of them, since your health and life might be at stake. You want a doctor and pharmacist who believe in truth, a fixed standard of reality that guides their decisions.

The problem is that many people who insist on living by truth in the physical realm confidently reject it in the spiritual realm. But simply announcing that truth does not exist does not solve anything. We are faced with this thing called truth, and we have to do something with it.

Pontius Pilate asked the question of the ages when truth Incarnate in the person of Jesus Christ stood before him on trial. Jesus said to Pilate, "For this I have been born, and for this I have come into the world, to testify to the truth. Everyone who is of the truth hears My voice" (John 18:37).

Pilate responded, "What is truth?" (v. 38).

If that evil Roman governor had been an honest seeker, he would have found the answer to his question. In fact, Jesus had definitively answered Pilate's question the night before at the Last Supper, during His prayer to the Father on our behalf: "Sanctify them in the truth; Your word is truth" (John 17:17). The Bible is truth—the whole truth and nothing but the truth.

The world has always been confused and divided on the

question of truth. There has been a myriad of responses to the question, "What is truth?" The *denier*, for lack of a better term, is the person who simply dismisses and rejects the very concept of truth.

The *agnostic* says that absolute knowledge on issues, such as God's existence, cannot be attained in this life. Since the word *agnostic* means "without knowledge," the agnostic's answer to Pilate's question would be, "I don't know." This person is supposedly the perpetual questioner and seeker after truth.

The *rationalist* says that human reason and experience are the ultimate criteria for determining truth. Rationalism focuses on the mind and simply says that whatever the mind conceives of as being reality is, in fact, truth. Rationalism thus limits the search for truth. It is one of the theories that came into play during the eighteenth-century movement known as the Enlightenment when the truths upon which Christianity is based came under sustained attack and were largely abandoned.

There is also a school of thought called *positivism*, which says truth is limited to that which can be validated by the scientific method. If science authenticates a theory, then perhaps we can regard it as truth. Positivism doesn't leave any room for a supernatural Savior with a supernatural revelation, because these things cannot be tested by the scientific method in a lab.

Another of mankind's many answers to the question of truth is *relativism*, which says that truth is subjective and personal. Truth is what we feel at the moment to be true, so therefore what's true for me may not be true for you.

Pragmatism is yet another means of seeking to arrive at truth. Pragmatism appeals to a lot of people because it claims that truth is whatever works. This approach is tailor-made for our American love of a "my truth" thinking that says we are each entitled to our own version of truth.

I need to mention one other significant route people have taken in attempts to arrive at truth. This is man-made religion, defined as humanity's best attempts to reach up to and understand God—or even deny that He exists or cares about what happens to us. The *religionist* may be the hardest person of all to deal with, because he claims to be a follower of God and a seeker of spiritual truth. But more often than not, religion denies the absolute truth that God has spoken with finality in Jesus Christ (see Heb. 1:1–2) by requiring that which is not revealed in God's Word.

I am not saying that people cannot discover certain truths on their own. But the problem with the world's "truth" is that it often has to be revised or discarded when new facts are uncovered. Hundreds of years ago, people were convinced the earth was flat. People feared that if explorers sailed to the edge of the earth, they might fall off. But that "truth" had to be discarded as new evidence was found.

How about a contemporary example of changing truth? If you follow the world of nutrition and health today, your head is probably spinning trying to keep up with all of the new, and sometimes conflicting, information about the content and value of certain foods.

Since research is constantly ongoing, today's facts may be tomorrow's myths. And, from a biblical standpoint, we can't trust our moral instincts to determine truth, because we have been corrupted by sin. Our intellect is also a poor guide to truth, because we are finite creatures whose knowledge is extremely limited.

The only reason we can know any truth at all is because God is God. Truth is not just that which conforms to reality, because there is no reality apart from God. Truth is that which conforms to His nature. We as Christians can make an unapologetic, uncompromising, definitive statement about truth because of the perfectly true nature of God. The Bible calls God the Father "Him who is true" (1 John 5:20), and Jesus made the astounding statement, "I am the way, and the *truth*, and the life" (John 14:6, emphasis added).

Here's one example of the way God's nature is the standard for what is true. The Bible says, "God is not a man, that He should lie" (Num. 23:19). Lying is wrong not just because it messes up people and causes harm, but because it violates God's very nature. The same can be said for murder and theft and adultery and coveting. These actions are out of line with

God's character. Truth and purity are part of His eternal attributes.

So while our current culture may often say truth is whatever we want to make it, God says truth must conform to a fixed standard. If I gave you a sheet of paper and a pencil and asked you to draw a straight line freehand, no matter how meticulous you were, your line would not be truly straight. But if I gave you a ruler with a sharp edge to draw your line against, the outcome would be totally different. So long as your pencil follows that fixed standard, your line will be straight. And anyone else can take that same ruler and make a straight line, too. Since God is by nature true, in order for something to be true, it must conform to Him and His written revelation.

Inspiration

God safeguarded the truth of His Word through the process called divine inspiration. As seen earlier, the apostle Peter, who experienced this inspiration, said the Holy Spirit oversaw the writing of Scripture so that there was no contamination in it (see 2 Peter 1:20–21). This is why we can say that God is the Bible's true Author.

But even though the Bible's human authors were "moved" or "carried along" by the Holy Spirit, they often appealed to their own experiences and witness as reliable. Peter said, "We did not follow cleverly devised tales when we made known to you the power and coming of our Lord Jesus Christ, but we were eyewitnesses of His majesty" (2 Peter 1:16). Peter went on to relate the transfiguration of Jesus, which Peter saw and heard (vv. 17–18). John, another apostolic eyewitness, wrote about "what we have heard" and "what we have seen with our eyes" (1 John 1:1).

The writers of Scripture were safeguarded by the Holy Spirit from error; He moved them to write and equipped them in the process. These men were so convinced of the divine truth that they were willing to die for it.

Suppose I were part of a conspiracy to say that Jesus was the Son of God and had risen from the dead even if I knew such a claim was a lie. If people said they would kill me for holding such a belief, I'd show them where the body was. It wouldn't make sense to die for something I knew to be false. But the writers of Scripture stood by the Word even when it meant they would be killed.

Inerrancy

We have said that the Bible is the complete truth, and now I want to give you an important term for this doctrine, which you may already be familiar with. That word is *inerrant*, which means "without error." Fundamentally, inerrancy means that God's Word forms an absolutely fixed, firm foundation of truth. Some people will say the Bible contains truth or contains the Word of God. But that's only half the truth, because it leaves open the possibility that the Bible also contains other things. The inerrancy of Scripture means that the Bible is true no matter what the subject. It is free from error.

Some Bible critics are quick to point out that the existing manuscripts we have of the Bible vary one from another in numerous places. So, the argument goes that we can't talk about the Bible being inerrant because we don't have the original manuscripts, also called the autographs.

One objection to this argument has to do with human nature: God knows that if we had the original autographs of Scripture, we would be tempted to make an idol out of them and worship them instead of their Author. That would be a sin, of course. If you don't think humans have an incurable need to make something visible to worship, go to Israel and see all the religious shrines with ornate altars and thousands of lights and candles that various Christian groups have built over the centuries at holy sites.

But what about the objection that the transmission of content from the autographs to the works after them had to pass through the hands of humanity, thus leaving open the door for error? When we measure this process against the common critical standards of historically viable documents, we find that the text of the Scripture surpasses all others.

First, handwritten transmission has been a trusted historical process for centuries. While it may first come as a shock, most of what we know from both secular and religious ancient history is fundamentally dependent upon the reliability of handwritten transmission of texts. In fact, readily available printed manuscripts were not in circulation until the invention of the movable type printing press in the fifteenth century. This means that what we know of ancient Egypt, Greek, and Roman history, and of the Middle Ages up until the time of the Reformation, is solely dependent upon accurate scribal transmission of written texts.

Second, the process of copying handwritten manuscripts was extremely meticulous and safeguarded the purity of the text. The Old Testament had several different scribal traditions and text families spanning the thousands of years of its writing and transmission. Several textbooks guided scribes to accurately transmit the Scriptures. One is called the *Oklah we-Oklah* and contained more than four hundred lists covering various details of words and verses that are easily confused, giving instructions on how to tell them apart. The Masoretic tradition also provided a method of accenting the written text and adding vowels (the original Hebrew text was written in all consonants) that made the traditional reading of the text more systematic and easier to transmit correctly.

Also, commentaries existed in the margins or at the end of manuscripts for the purpose of guiding future readers and copyists on how best to read, write, and understand the Scripture. One example is the *Masorah finalis*, a commentary at the end of books or sections of books that detailed how many individual words were in a book. This simplified the proofing of a finished manuscript so that the reviewer could determine that a new copy had the exact number of letters as the original. At times, it even indicated the middle word or consonant of a book for easy cross referencing between the original and the copied manuscripts.[2]

Lastly, scribes were very cautious, recognizing the warning of the Scriptures against tampering with or distorting the Holy Scriptures (Deut. 4:1–2; 12:28, 32; Prov. 30:5–6, Rev. 22:18–19).

Supposed Contradictions

The reason we still affirm the Bible's inerrancy in the autographs, even though we don't have them, is that it is absolutely crucial to believe and know that we have a perfect standard to work against as we compare the various existing manuscripts. Where the texts of biblical manuscripts differ, scholars work to reach the closest consensus possible on what the original said. And while these examples can be particularly disorienting for Christians, since they come from the very text of Scripture itself, these apparent contradictions can be addressed by looking at the context of these passages and the intention of the writers.

---

2. Ellis R. Brotzman, *Old Testament Textual Criticism: A Practical Introduction* (Grand Rapids, MI: Baker Academic, 1994), 50–53.

Let's look at two examples of the most commonly cited "contradictions." First, the use of the Old Testament in the New Testament. Various passages of the Old Testament are paraphrased in the New Testament. In certain cases it appears there are differences in the language and tension between the original text and the way it is being used in the New Testament.

When addressing this challenge, keep in mind that the biblical authors of the New Testament were utilizing a translation of the Old Testament called the Septuagint. The Septuagint (sometimes abbreviated as "LXX" because of the seventy translators who were believed to have worked on it together) is the Greek version of the Old Testament compiled in the third century BC once Greek had become the common trade language of the ancient world. It was this version of the Old Testament that most first-century Jews, including Jesus and His disciples, would have read and memorized.

One example of the differences this can create between the Hebrew Old Testament and the New Testament's use of the Septuagint can be seen in Acts 2:25–28, where Peter quotes a famous passage from Psalm 16:8–11. The differences in these passages are partially the result of the LXX translation that Peter uses word for word. Some scholars believe that some changes, like "my flesh will also live in hope" (the LXX and Peter's quote) as opposed to "my flesh also will dwell securely" (the Old Testament text based on the

Hebrew), may account for Peter's application of this passage to Jesus' resurrection (see Acts 2:29–32).

Often the differences between the Hebrew version and the Septuagint can be accounted for in much of the same way as the two different English versions. The act of translation always comes with choices about which words to use, how to arrange the words, and how well a word translated into a new culture or time period. Yet the goal of a translator is to remain faithful to the intent of the original passage.

The comparison of this text from Psalm 16 and Acts 2 reveals that the changes are only minor variations in the language or the way a concept is expressed, and they bear little impact on our understanding of the inerrancy of Scripture. However, Peter's use of Psalm 16 does bring to light how the early Christians read all Old Testament texts through the new lens of their fulfillment in Christ. Since Christ had come to fulfill the Old Testament (see Matt. 5:17; Luke 24:40–44), particular words and passages took on new light and meaning that could be seen only in light of Christ's coming. The early Christians took these Old Testament Scriptures as authentic, truthful, inerrant texts that witnessed to Christ's coming.

Another challenge to inerrancy highlights differences between various passages that report the same event or teaching, but in different ways. These differences are sometimes cited as a proof that Scripture contradicts itself and thus cannot be inerrant. One of the most well-known examples of this regards the exact time of Jesus' crucifixion. Mark and John both mention the hour, and these times seem to contradict (see Mark 15:22–25 and John 19:14–15). Several theories have been given that can harmonize the accounts in Mark and John.

One possible explanation for the differences in times is the close resemblance of the Greek script for the numbers three (Γ) and six (F). Mark's gospel suggests that the crucifixion occurred at the third hour which would be considered 9:00 a.m. John's gospel cites the time of the final trial to be at the sixth hour, which would suggest that Jesus was crucified at noon.

Another explanation is that John utilized the Roman system of time keeping, whereas Mark used a Jewish system. Others conclude that Mark and John were both using approximations for the time of Jesus' crucifixion, and the events surrounding it. Both writers, however, have in common that the event occurred in the late morning hours.

While we cannot fully account for the harmonization of these two accounts, we can conclude that the contrast between them is not so significant that they would impact our commitment to inerrancy. Both accounts point to the same situation with clarity and striking similarity with other accounts of Jesus' death (see Matt. 27:2, 11–14; Mark 15:1b–5; Luke 23:1–5; John 18:29–38).

Many of these so-called contradictions can be accounted

for if we carefully read and study these texts in more detail, and rely on the help of conservative scholars who are also committed to inerrancy.

THE AUTHORITY OF GOD'S VOICE

The supreme kind of authority that a king holds over his subjects by virtue of his office, the Bible holds by virtue of its Author, who is the King of creation and Ruler over all the earth. The Bible's authority is inherent in its every word and even every portion of a word. The Bible is also supremely authoritative because it is God's revelation in history.

The Bible is God's voice in print, meaning that the words of Scripture come from His mouth. This is the doctrine of inspiration, which we'll consider later. Christians talk about hearing God's voice in His Word, or hearing God speak to them through His Word. This is the Holy Spirit's ministry of illumination, which we will also look at later.

The term "God's voice" will help us grasp what we might call the immediacy of the Bible's authority. That is, the Bible's authority is timeless. For example, when we read in Exodus 20:3, "You shall have no other gods before Me," this command has the very same force behind it today that it had when God first thundered these words to Moses more than three thousand years ago. This is important because one problem I see as a pastor—and you may see as well—is that people disregard God's Word because they believe it's just ink on a page.

Receiving the Bible as God's voice speaking directly to us is important because of another common problem among God's people. This shows up when people know what God said, and can even repeat it back to you, but they aren't doing anything about it. Every parent is familiar with this scenario. Your child disregards your direct instructions, and when you confront that child later and say, "What did I tell you to do?" he or she can repeat your words verbatim. But for some reason your command didn't carry any weight with that child, so the result was disobedience. And a good parent won't let that go without appropriate discipline (see Heb. 12:5–6).

Our heavenly Father has spoken to us in His Word. He has told us what to do, how to think, and how to live. Scripture is God's voice in print. So when we preach from the Bible, we need to emphasize the authoritative nature of His Word in order that those who listen will apply the truths from the Word to their own lives.

Jesus was being challenged by His opponents one day when He tried to tell them that He was God. They objected, accused Him of blasphemy, and even got ready to stone Him (see John 10:31–33). Jesus turned to Scripture to make His case, and the way He used the Word teaches us much about the Bible's authority.

Jesus answered them, "Has it not been written in your Law, 'I said, you are gods'? If he called them gods, to whom the word of God came (*and the Scripture cannot be broken*), do you say of Him, whom the Father sanctified and sent into the world, 'You are blaspheming,' because I said, 'I am the Son of God'?" (vv. 34–36, emphasis added)

Jesus was using a powerful argument here. He said that if the Bible—in this case the psalmist Asaph (Ps. 82:6)—used the term "gods" for men who were merely God's representatives, then those who were accusing Jesus should not object if He called Himself God. Why? Because they had just seen Him heal a blind man (John 9) and do other miracles, for one thing.

What I want you to see here is the binding authority of Scripture. Not even one word can be changed. Scripture is irrefragable, which means it cannot be voided or invalidated. How important is this trait? It was important enough to Jesus that He built a critical argument around it.

The Lord's opponents might have wished they could nullify or get around the word *gods* in Psalm 82:6, because it is the Hebrew word *elohim*, which is one of the names of God. But Jesus had them, because God's Word called His representatives "gods," and nothing could change the Scripture.

Paul used a similar tactic in Galatians 3 to prove that

Jesus is Abraham's promised seed. The validity of Paul's entire point hung on the difference between the singular "seed" and the plural "seeds" (v. 16). Not only each letter of the Bible, but even the smallest part of each letter (see Matt. 5:18) is vital and carries God's authority.

Jesus Christ also said that the Bible carries the imprint of His divine authority. He announced to His disciples, "Heaven and earth will pass away, but My words will not pass away" (Matt. 24:35). That statement on the lips of anyone other than Jesus would be blasphemy, but He alone can claim, "All authority has been given to Me in heaven and on earth" (Matt. 28:18). Therefore, Jesus' words recorded in Scripture will outlast history, because the Word is eternal. I love the way the psalmist put it: "Forever, O LORD, Your word is settled in heaven" (Ps. 119:89).

Since Jesus possesses all authority, and His Word has all His authority behind it, why are members of the churches we pastor not seeing God's Word at work? I am convinced the reason is that they are not living as though God's Word is our authority, and we are not continually teaching it. We are not seeing more power in our lives and in our churches because we aren't taking the Bible seriously.

The fact that the Bible is completely authoritative and cannot be broken is a wonderful doctrine of the Christian faith. But the truth and power of God's Word can be nullified in your experience if you refuse to let the Word speak to you as it is or if you start mixing it with your human viewpoints.

Now please notice that I did not say the Bible can lose its power or authority. That will never happen, because God said His Word is "settled in heaven." But the Bible's power is blunted in our lives when we do not respond to God in humility and obedience.

This is probably the number one travesty that people who claim to believe and follow God's Word commit against it. Many people who mix their own thoughts with the Bible's teaching have many degrees after their name. Education is fine, and the church has benefited from well-trained commentators and scholars who seek to understand and communicate to others what the Word means. But there's a big difference between an honest attempt to understand the Bible and diluting its teachings with human thinking. The best example of this is in Scripture itself, when the Pharisees and scribes came to Jesus to accuse His disciples of breaking "the tradition of the elders" (Matt. 15:1–2).

But Jesus came back at them with a far more serious charge, that of nullifying the Word of God (vv. 4–6), using the example of God's commandment to honor one's father and mother. Jesus showed how the scribes and Pharisees allowed people, mainly themselves, to get around this clear command with a hollow promise to give those resources to God while actually not having to give them away at all.

Jesus identified their problem when He said at the end

of verse 6, "And by this you invalidated the word of God for the sake of your tradition." God never meant for the commandment to honor your father and mother to be skirted on a technicality. The Pharisees added so many traditions and regulations to the Law that they ended up creating a barrier around the Word so people couldn't get to it.

The Bible says, "Let God be found true, though every man be found a liar" (Rom. 3:4). The issue Jesus dealt with was the authority of God's Word. If God says we are to honor our parents, then trying to find a loophole in that command is a sin against the truth—and God.

This issue of truth and authority is at the core of why the Holy Spirit is not doing more in our lives. The Spirit is the Spirit of truth who is obligated to God's Word. So, when we start diluting the Word with our human viewpoints, the Spirit steps back, because He is not going to bless our speculations.

There's an interesting story in 2 Kings 4:38–41 about the prophet Elisha and the "apprentice prophets" who were under his tutelage. There was a famine in the land, and these student prophets were hungry. Elisha told his servant to make a pot of stew for everybody, and one of the prophets gathered some wild gourds for the stew. The gourds looked fine to him, and he probably thought they would add a little spice to the stew. So, he decided to help out by tossing the gourds into the stew. But as everyone ate, some apparently began to feel sick and said the stew was poisoned. Someone cried out to Elisha, "O man of God, there is death in the pot" (v. 40). Elisha took care of the problem, and the stew was fine.

Unfortunately, this happens every Sunday in churches all across this nation. Plenty of pastors and teachers are tossing "wild gourds" into the pot—adding human wisdom to God's Word or even allowing human views and opinions to replace the Scriptures. This is why people can actually be worse off by going to church, because they come away more confused and unsure than ever about whether the Bible is true, let alone whether it has any relevance for them. Remember, a mist in the pulpit creates a fog in the pew.

Biblical authority means staying true to God's truth alone. It also means that God has the supreme right to determine our decision making and set the agenda for our lives. God doesn't want our rationalizations, but our response.

Paul told Timothy to preach the Word whether it was convenient or not because people would want to have "their ears tickled" instead of hearing the truth (2 Tim. 4:2–3). There's nothing wrong with preaching in such a way that your congregants leave feeling good, so long as the authoritative truth of God's inerrant Word is what makes them feel good.

CHAPTER TWO

SUFFICIENCY

◆

The Word of God can transform any situation or person because built into it is the ability to pull off whatever God desires it to accomplish. Power is the ability to effect change or produce the desired effect. This is a good working definition of what I mean by the power of God's Word.

A key Scripture passage that teaches this truth is in Isaiah 55. Verse 11 says, "So will My word be which goes forth from My mouth; it will not return to Me empty, without accomplishing what I desire, and without succeeding in the matter for which I sent it."

The unstoppable power of God's Word sets it apart from anyone else's word.

Unlike our words, God's Word cannot be frustrated or stopped. His Word is always purposeful when it goes out from His mouth, and that purpose is always achieved. God's power is never random or out of control. God always has a plan that He intends to fulfill. Let's look at the power of God's Word as it relates to *creation* and *the soul*.

GOD'S WORD SUFFICIENT FOR CREATION

When the writers of Scripture want to illustrate the awesome power of God, they often point to His creation. The psalmist declares, "By the word of the LORD the heavens were made, and by the breath of His mouth all their host" (Ps. 33:6). Then he adds in verse 9, "For He spoke, and it was done; He commanded, and it stood fast," referring to the earth and all its mighty oceans.

To speak a world into existence is power beyond anything we can imagine. Genesis 1 records again and again that "God said . . . and it was so." This is creation *ex nihilo*, making not just *something* out of nothing, but *everything* out of nothing. No human being can accomplish this. But God speaks two words in the Hebrew text of Genesis 1:3, which could be translated "Light be," and light appears. He speaks again, and the dry land appears. Time after time, God says the word, and whatever He commands comes into being. God simply works out His will through His Word.

I like the way Paul puts it. He says that God "calls into being that which does not exist" (Rom. 4:17). The apostle emphasizes God's power in the middle of discussing Abraham's faith in God's promise to give him a child—even though he and Sarah were way too old to become parents. In fact, the Bible says that in terms of their ability to bear children, both Sarah and Abraham were as good as dead (v. 19). That is no problem for God. His word to Abraham is, "I will surely return to you at this time next year; and behold, Sarah your wife will have a son" (Gen. 18:10).

The power of God's Word is on display in an even greater way in the birth of Jesus Christ, who is *the* promised Son (of which Isaac, Abraham and Sarah's son, was a type). Luke 1:26–38 is an incredible passage of Scripture that tells of the angel Gabriel announcing to Mary that she was going to have a baby. You know the rest of the story. Gabriel informs Mary that she will be with child by the Holy Spirit, so the One she bears will be a miraculous child. If God can plant His eternal, pre-existent Son in a virgin's womb, then nothing is impossible for Him. No word that God speaks is impossible for Him to accomplish. This means it doesn't matter who tries to stop God from carrying out the Word He has spoken. The enemy can throw up all sorts of defenses and may even appear to be winning sometimes, because God allows human choices and failings to be part of His plan. But God guarantees that even those things will be incorporated into His divine program. No matter how long it takes or what has to happen, God will accomplish His objective. His Word is sure and effective.

God not only brought the universe into *existence* by the power of His Word, but also *sustains* His creation by that same Word. The writer of Hebrews says of Jesus, "He is the radiance of [God's] glory and the exact representation of His nature, and upholds all things by the word of His power" (1:3). God sustains what He brings into being (see 2 Peter 3:5–7). This is part of the good news of our salvation. The reason you can't lose your salvation is that what God creates, He keeps. Every Christian is a new creation in Christ (see 2 Cor. 5:17), and no one can snatch them from God's hand (see John 10:28–30).

GOD'S WORD SUFFICIENT FOR THE SOUL

From the vastness of creation to the inner workings of the human soul and spirit, God's Word is over all. When a person believes in Christ, their spirit, which is their capacity to relate to God, is made alive by the Holy Spirit. The soul is the self-life, or the human identity—your mind, emotions, and will. God's Word has the power to pierce into the deepest recesses of our being with laser-like power and precision. We know this from a great passage of Scripture that I hope is familiar to you:

> For the word of God is living and active and sharper than any two-edged sword, and piercing as far as the

division of soul and spirit, of both joints and marrow, and able to judge the thoughts and intentions of the heart. And there is no creature hidden from His sight, but all things are open and laid bare to the eyes of Him with whom we have to do. (Heb. 4:12–13)

The Bible is not dead words on a page, but is alive and powerful, which is the idea behind the word *active.* The Bible is a living document because it is the Word of the living God, animated by the living Holy Spirit. Genesis 1:2 says that God's Spirit was "moving," or hovering, over the waters of the earth at creation, breathing life into creation.

The Holy Spirit does the same thing with the Word that He did with creation. The Spirit is intimately connected with the Word and brings it alive to hearers and readers, with the result that we are not to read the Bible the way we read a novel or a history book. We read other books to get information or to be entertained, but we should read the Bible to receive life from it and allow it to penetrate our hearts, the inner core of our being.

People may ask you how they can know when the Bible is really beginning to come alive to them. Your answer should be simple. You know the Bible is alive when it begins to go to work in your life and transform you because that's what Hebrews 4:12 says the Word is designed to do. It changes and conforms you to the image of Christ. The writer of Hebrews likened the Bible to a two-edged sword that cuts on both sides as it is thrust into the target. Roman soldiers carried these swords, which were kept very sharp. When a Roman soldier used his two-edged sword on an enemy, it penetrated deeply for maximum effect.

Now, if this imagery seems a little graphic to you, then you're getting the idea. God's Word is so sharp and powerful that it can plunge into us like a sharp sword that cuts not even just to the bone, but into the marrow inside the bone. No other book can reach down into a person that deeply and bring about the effects that the Bible can.

In other words, God wants His Word to perform spiritual surgery on us. He wants it to reveal what is in us to us. The Bible says, "The heart is more deceitful than all else and is desperately sick; who can understand it?" (Jer. 17:9). The answer is that no one can understand the human heart perfectly—no one, that is, except God. He knows our deepest thoughts because we are completely exposed before Him.

This explains why people testify that when they read the Bible, they feel as if it is looking into the deepest recesses of their minds and hearts. It's a good thing to be probed and exposed by the incision that God makes in our lives by His Word, because that's when we really deal with deep-rooted sin and begin to grow.

Make no mistake about it. One of the riskiest things you can do is give the Holy Spirit permission to open you up and do spiritual surgery on you. But it's also one of the most important things you can do, and must do, for the same reason that it's important to give your doctor permission to operate on you when you have a physical issue. It isn't until you submit to the surgeon's knife that real healing can take place. And it isn't until you are personally transformed by the Word of God that you can discover your own spiritual healing that will then enable you to shepherd others into a similar experience of spiritual healing.

It's amazing that medical science has such sophisticated equipment that doctors can look inside a human heart while it is beating to see what's going on. A skilled heart specialist doesn't just look into your heart like an impartial observer who simply records what he sees without making any judgments or decisions. The doctor critiques, or evaluates, the situation based on what his examination reveals. Hebrews 4:12 says that God's Word does something similar. It critiques "the thoughts and intentions of the heart."

We may assume that most of our thoughts and intentions are fine, but ultimately we are incapable of making that judgment. We need the Holy Spirit to take the sword of the Word and slice us open right down to the core of our being, to separate what is good from what is worthless. Through the power of God's Word, you will come to see yourself as God sees you. You will also come to see God in ways that you could not see Him otherwise.

God's purpose is for His Word to remake us from the inside out, conforming us to the image of Christ (see Rom. 8:29; 2 Cor. 3:17–18). Thus, the power of God's Word is discovered as we cooperate with the purposes for which God gave us His Word. The Word will always accomplish God's will, which is good and perfect (see Rom. 12:2).

As pastors, it is our duty to get the Word of God to as many people as possible so that the Word can do the work it's designed to do. Pastor, if you do not get people to engage with God's Word through your sermons, you are not doing your job. Find another calling. Because you have been chosen as an instrument through whom God distributes the truths in His Word. People have to pay attention to learn and hear. If they are not paying attention to you, then you need to find ways to keep their attention because nothing is more important than the transference of God's Word to a world in need.

GOD'S WORD IS
SUFFICIENT FOR EVERYTHING

The Bible's sufficiency means that God's Word is comprehensive in its ability to speak to every area and every need in life. There is no life issue we will ever face that is not addressed either by direct command or by general principle in the Word. God has given us "everything pertaining to life and godliness" (2 Peter 1:3).

I've been preaching the Bible for over fifty years, yet I have only begun to tap into the endless vein of truth of God's Word. Every time I go to the Word, there is something new I didn't see before, something deep I didn't understand. The Bible is inexhaustible in scope, and thus sufficient for life.

Someone has said that while the Bible is so deep that theologians can spend a lifetime plumbing its depths, it is so simple a child can read and understand it. The sufficiency of Scripture is such that every age can learn from its teachings. Paul put this doctrine into a compact statement when he wrote: "All Scripture is inspired by God and profitable for teaching [or doctrine], for reproof, for correction, for training [or instruction] in righteousness; so that the man of God may be adequate, equipped for every good work" (2 Tim. 3:16–17).

Psalm 19:7–14 lays out the sufficiency of the Word in very beautiful and clear terms. Therein, the psalmist David makes multiple statements about the ability of God's revelation to address every area of human existence and, in particular, every area that we as believers need to know to please God. These verses also speak to the all-consuming desire we should have for the Word and remind us that God's Word can keep us from sin.

Verses 1–6 of Psalm 19 form a backdrop to this poetic tribute to the Word, and we need to review them briefly. They deal with general revelation: the evidence of God "written" into every atom of creation and made available to every person.

The psalm begins with a declaration: "The heavens are telling of the glory of God; and their expanse is declaring the work of His hands" (v. 1). In other words, even someone who can't read or doesn't have a Bible can still know beyond a doubt that there is a God. The reality of God ought to be clear simply by observing the world around us. The Bible never spends time defending God's existence, but says instead, "The fool has said in his heart, 'There is no God'" (Ps. 14:1). People have to be taught not to believe in God, because it is natural for human beings to look around them and above them and conclude that someone bigger and more powerful than they made all of this. It's also natural for people to worship or at least try to placate the higher being they know is there.

Just reading Psalm 19:1–6 makes it clear that God's revelation of Himself in creation is powerful and profound. But general revelation is also limited. It is enough to condemn the sinner, as Paul said in Romans 1:18–23. In fact, those who reject or pervert this witness in nature are "without excuse" (v. 20) because they did not follow it to its logical conclusion, which is to seek the God of whom it speaks.

But general revelation is limited because it is not sufficient in and of itself to save the sinner. Psalm 19:3 says of the heavens as God's witness, "There is no speech, nor are there words; their voice is not heard." We can look at the stars or the oceans and know that the creator God must be great and powerful. But we must go to His Word to learn that He has spoken to us.

We can be eternally grateful that Psalm 19 does not end with verse 6—or that Romans 1 does not contain only condemnation, for that matter. Let's consider this psalm's numerous declarations and descriptions about the glorious sufficiency of God's Word.

God's Word is perfect and restorative. David began this hymn of praise by saying, "The law of the LORD is perfect, restoring the soul" (v. 7a). "Law" is another term for the Scripture. David must have wanted to begin with the most important aspect because he described the Word of God as perfect—that which is whole, complete, not lacking in any area. The Bible is complete in its revelation of divine truth.

The second half of this phrase in Psalm 19:7a shows us the benefit of His perfect Word: it restores the soul. This is a picture of something being brought back to its original condition, being revived or refreshed. The Bible is sufficient to take what is broken and restore it, much like you might restore an old piece of furniture to its original beauty.

What is the soul? The Hebrew word *nephesh* refers to the essence of your being, who you are at your core. Your soul is you, your essence. It comprises not only your mind, but also your emotions and your will. When a person dies, that soul will either go to heaven or to hell. The key to experiencing transformation in Christ takes place within our soul because our soul is what has been created for eternity.

The problem with our souls is that they have been contaminated since birth, making them distorted. Have you ever been to an amusement park and seen the mirrors that make you look fat, super-skinny, tall, short, or crooked? This is what has happened to our souls. To varying degrees, the effects of sin have engrafted themselves into our souls. The soul needs to be fixed, but the soul can't fix itself.

Most of the time, we are trying to get the soul to fix the soul, but that works just about as well as getting distortion to fix distortion. I call this approach soul management. It's not the restoration the psalmist spoke of. Rather, soul management is when we spend time, energy, and money trying to make our souls better. We make resolutions and promises that are tied to the soul and its influence on our body. We determine that we will spend more time in God's Word, cut back on unhealthy foods, or stop watching entertainment that negatively influences us, among other things. We need to be especially careful that we don't focus on soul management. It may help for a while, but only true restoration is lasting.

Only God can bring about restoration through the power of His Word. Jesus died on the cross not just to take your soul to heaven, but also to deliver your soul in history. And when Jesus returns, your soul will be fully restored.

God's Word gives wisdom. David goes on to make a second statement about the Word of God in verse seven:

"The testimony of the LORD is sure, making wise the simple" (v. 7b). God's testimony refers to His truth as revealed in Scripture. Only God's witness is one hundred percent true, because He Himself is one hundred percent true. Thus, His Word is completely solid, or trustworthy. You can build your life on it. That's what the psalmist meant when he said the Word is "sure," like a rock, as opposed to something unstable and flimsy.

Jesus used this contrast in His famous parable of the wise man who built his house on the rock and the foolish man who built on sand (see Matt. 7:24–27). The rock held firm in the storm, while the sand gave way because it was ultimately an unreliable foundation. The difference between the two men was whether they heeded or ignored His Word. That's what makes a person wise in the biblical sense. Wisdom is the application of biblical truth to your life, to build your life intentionally on God's Word, so you're ready when the storms hit. Until our belief in the living Word is obeyed, it does not become activated in our experience (1 Thess. 2:13).

The pastor's ministry must be built on the foundation of biblical application. Jesus makes it clear that this is to be a foundational issue for building a house, and the local church is called God's household (1 Tim. 3:15; 1 Peter 2:5). Pastors serve as stewards over His house, and God has entrusted us with the sacred task of equipping God's people to bring their lives into conformity to God's Word.

James reiterates the importance of biblical application when he says that the blessing of God comes in the doing—not merely in the hearing, studying, memorizing, and learning—of Scripture (James 1:21–25). Failure of pastors to focus on the application of God's Word means that their ministries are being built on sand (applying human wisdom) and not on rock (applying divine wisdom), which means that both their ministries and the lives of their people will be weak and not strong when the storms of life hit. It also means that the people likely will be powerless to bring God's presence into their circumstances since the Word will not seem to be working for them. We need an ongoing growth in God's Word to guide us. Psalm 19 is a reminder that the Bible can save us a lot of heartache by giving us the ability to discern situations with godly wisdom and make God-honoring choices.

God's Word is right. "The precepts of the LORD are right, rejoicing the heart" (v. 8a). Here David described the Bible using a word that means the particulars of divine instruction. Sometimes God states explicitly what He does and does not want us to do, while at other times He gives us general principles that apply to a multitude of situations. Both are designed to govern our character and conduct, and both are equally authoritative. God's precepts just spell out things in more detail so that we can live a well-ordered life.

One example of a biblical precept is in Proverbs 6:1–5, where we are told not to become "surety," or what we would call a cosigner, for a stranger's debts. The reason is obvious: if the borrower defaults on the debt, we will be left holding the note and the debt. God's Word tells us by way of principle to be wise in how we handle our finances, but Proverbs 6 gets down to a specific case of avoiding the trap of guaranteeing someone else's debts.

The Lord's precepts are always on target. "Right" in Hebrew means to show someone the correct path, the right way, the road he or she ought to take. God's precepts are right even when nobody else agrees. The gospel is "foolishness" to the unsaved world (1 Cor. 1:21), but it is the right path to take. In following the right path, your heart rejoices through the abiding presence and provision of God. Your heart is also able to maintain that joy by being protected from experiencing the consequences of living in opposition to God's precepts. Jesus spoke about two roads: the broad road that is crowded but leads to destruction, and the narrow road that has plenty of room because there are so few people on it (see Matt. 7:13–14).

God's Word enables understanding. There is more good news in Psalm 19, because the Word tells us, "The commandment of the LORD is pure, enlightening the eyes" (v. 8b). "Commandment" means the Bible's teachings are divine mandates—they are not optional. God is not writing down suggestions for us to consider. Many people think the Bible contains Ten Commandments, but here David described all of God's revelation as a commandment that is binding on us.

The opposite of having our eyes spiritually enlightened is to have them darkened or blinded. Jesus prayed in Matthew 11:25, "I praise You, Father, Lord of heaven and earth, that You have hidden these things from the wise and intelligent and have revealed them to infants." The intelligent here are those who are wise in their own eyes and don't feel they need God's Word to enlighten them. But people who are dependent on God gain insight and wisdom as God opens their eyes to His will, thus guiding and directing their life path (see Eph. 1:18).

God's Word is clean. In verse 9 we read, "The fear of the LORD is clean, enduring forever." The word "clean" is similar to "pure" in that it speaks of an absence of impurity or defilement. God conveys His truth without flaw or blemish. Psalm 12:6 declares, "The words of the LORD are pure words . . . refined seven times."

The fear of the Lord is the reverential awe of God that the Bible inspires in those who love Him and seek to live by His commandments and precepts. Essentially, to fear God means to take Him seriously. The fear of God will last forever, because even when we are in heaven with Jesus, God will not lose any of His majesty, and we will not lose the awe in which He wants us to hold Him. In fact, our awe of the Lord will be infinitely increased when we are with Him in His uninterrupted, holy presence.

As the pure expression of God's heart and mind, the Bible will also last forever. "Forever, O LORD, Your word is settled in heaven" (Ps. 119:89). The Bible is permanent and always relevant. It will never go out of date or out of print.

God's Word is righteous. "The judgments of the LORD are true; they are righteous altogether" (v. 9b). Judgments refer to the ordinances or divine verdicts issued from the bench of the Supreme Judge of the earth. The Bible is our infallible standard for judging all of life's situations. Because the Bible is the unadulterated truth of God, you become right with God when you apply it.

God's Word is sweet. Psalm 19:10 says the Word of God is "sweeter also than honey and the drippings of the honeycomb." That means it is better than any dessert you can dream of. Have you ever read a passage that became sweet to you? In fact, a number of prophets including Ezekiel (Ezek. 3:1), Jeremiah (Jer. 15:16), and John the apostle (Rev. 10:10) are described as eating God's Word—which often tasted sweet, like honey—in order to then share that Word with God's people. That's why the Bible invites us to "taste and see that the LORD is good" (Ps. 34:8). We are not talking about just reading the Bible, but about tasting and savoring what God has said in such a way that when we speak of it to others, they delight in what they hear.

God's Word protects. In closing, verses 11–13 of Psalm 19 is where the psalmist continues with a tribute to the Bible's ability to protect believers from sin of every kind. These include "hidden faults" (v. 12), those deep-down flaws we may not always be aware of that can trip us up, and "presumptuous sins" (v. 13), those we plan and deliberately commit. David's goal in all this was to be "blameless" and "acquitted of great transgression."

The psalm closes with a great prayer that expressed David's desire to respond properly to the wonderful truth that God's Word was all he would ever need. "Let the words of my mouth and the meditation of my heart be acceptable in Your sight, O LORD, my rock and my Redeemer" (v. 14). Clearly, God's Word is sufficient for every area of life. As such, it should be the basis and bedrock of everything you teach, write, or proclaim as a pastor or leader.

Years ago, there was a commercial for Prego spaghetti sauce. A mother is cooking the spaghetti, and the pot is full of a vibrant, red spaghetti sauce. The aroma seems to be filling the house. The son comes up, looks at his mother cooking the sauce, and asks, "Mom, where are the mushrooms?"

She says, "It's in there."

"But what about the sausage?"

"Well, it's in there."

"What about the ripe tomatoes?"

"It's in there."

Prego's spaghetti sauce had kick and flavor because of what was inside. Every time the boy looked for something to explain what he smelled, his mother would reply, "It's in there."

If you are looking for victory, it's in the Bible. If you're looking for transformation, it's in there. If you're looking for power, it's in there. If you're looking for deliverance, it's in there. If you're looking for a brand new start or a way to lead someone to a brand-new start, it's already there. The Word has given you everything you need, and you can tap into it by careful study and application of its truths.

CHAPTER THREE

CANONICITY

———————— ◆ ————————

The canonicity of Scripture is a very important part of bibliology, the doctrine or study of the Bible. The word *canon* means "a rule or standard." It refers to a reed used for measuring things, much like a ruler today. The classic definition of *canon* in church life is "rule of faith." Over the centuries of church history, many denominations and church bodies have drawn up canons that help determine belief and practice for their people. The Roman Catholic Church has their own canon of Scripture as well as an extensive body of canon law that has been collected and revised over many centuries.

In the process of time, the word *canon* also came to mean a catalog or list—in this case, the authoritative list of books that make up the Bible. The process of and criteria for determining canonicity tells us how the writings of the Bible became recognized as the authoritative and inspired Word of God and how they were collected and preserved. This subject is as intriguing as it is important because the process by which the books of the Bible were included is an amazing story in itself. But my primary concern is the product that we have in our hands today—the thirty-nine Old Testament books and twenty-seven New Testament books—that make up God's inspired, inerrant Word.

Despite the official canonicity of Scripture, there exists several different lists of books that are considered by others to be part of the Bible. During the process, there were many other so-called gospels, epistles, and manuscripts—written around the same time as other books of the Bible—that did not make it into the Scriptures. But here's the bottom line: God spoke His Word and inspired people to record every word exactly as He wanted them. Then God preserved His Word and oversaw the process by which the sixty-six books of the Bible were assembled into the complete and authoritative collection of Scripture.

Thus, the first question that must be answered concerning the Bible's canonicity is how some writings were chosen to be included in Scripture while others were excluded. What the early church did was discern, under the guidance of the Holy Spirit, which books *already* carried the stamp of the Spirit's inspiration, and which did not. The determining authority for the canon of Scripture was God Himself, not any church body or individual leader. God decided the canon of Scripture; people simply recognized it.

Let me give you an everyday example of what we're talking about. Suppose you sell something during your Saturday garage sale for one hundred dollars. On Monday, you go down to your bank to deposit the five crisp, new twenty-dollar bills the buyer gave you on Saturday, but to your horror, the bank teller informs you that all of the bills are counterfeit.

Now, after you recover your breath, you can protest all you want and remind her that you accepted the bills in good faith. You can say that the buyer seemed as honest as Abe Lincoln and even claimed to be a close friend of the bank's president. You can show the teller that the fake bills all have Andrew Jackson's picture on them, just like the other twenty-dollar bills in her till. You can even gather all the customers in the bank around and take a vote on whether the bills look and feel authentic to them. But none of that matters because you are still going to be out one hundred dollars. The fact is that the standard for authentic US bills has already been determined, and yours don't meet the standard.

Now, transfer this scenario to the Bible. Let's consider the book of Matthew, which was written by one of Jesus' twelve apostles. There was also a text floating around in the early church that claimed to be a "gospel" written by the apostle Thomas, who was just as authentic an apostle as Matthew.

How did the early church know that the gospel of Matthew was part of God's authentic revelation while the gospel of Thomas was not? And how can we be sure today that we're not missing something God wanted in the Bible?

The answer is that the church ran both books under the criteria of the Holy Spirit's sovereign guidance and direction, and the gospel of Thomas didn't last. Church leaders examined the books carefully for internal evidence of inspiration and checked the external evidence for their authenticity, following specific criteria—which we will look at in a moment—by which a book claiming to be Scripture either authenticated or disqualified itself.

We must understand this fundamental principle that God the Holy Spirit, and not man, determined the canon of Scripture. If we do not believe and affirm that the God who guided human beings to write Scripture also guided other human beings to collect it into one book, then our entire doctrine of Scripture crumbles like a house of cards. Why? Because God is perfect and His ways are perfect.

True, the very nature of ratifying one book and rejecting another created an element of human interaction with the text in which criteria had to be established and discerning judgments made. However, there is a difference between discerning what is already true versus making autonomous decisions about what can be true.

People did not have the authority to decide what is

Scripture, but God did allow, through the guidance of the Holy Spirit, individuals to participate in discerning which books God had already decided and designed to authentically reveal who He is. The church only recognized the canon that God established. That's a very important distinction, because if man determines what is Scripture, then man can add to it or take away from it.

Canonicity is not just a musty issue from ancient history, though. American founding father Thomas Jefferson, who was a deist, took a pair of scissors to the Gospels and cut out the parts he didn't accept. *The Da Vinci Code*, a popular novel (and later film) written by Dan Brown in 2003, highlighted several pseudepigraphal works—texts whose claimed authors are not the true authors, or works whose real authors attributed the work to a figure in the past—and brought them to the attention of the general public. Though Brown's book was a novel, some of his fictional assertions became mainstream. Brown suggested Leonardo da Vinci's famous *The Last Supper* was coded by the artist to point to Jesus having been married to Mary Magdalene. He brought to his audience's minds the supposed "gospel of Philip" and the "gospel of Mary" that allude to this relationship.

Brown suggested that these "gospels," among others, were hidden and unearthed among the Dead Sea Scrolls. However, the Dead Sea Scrolls found at Qumran did not contain any New Testament documents. In fact, the scribes at Qumran were a part of a Jewish sect that copied and preserved Scripture long before the birth of Christ. Because most people are unaware of that and the process of determining the canon, these books gained worldwide attention following Brown's assertion. The result was many people began to read these pseudepigraphal works as Scripture, causing some to question the legitimacy of the biblical canon.

Yet there are reasons why these books were not recorded as Scripture. Let's look at some of these now.

ADMISSION STANDARDS

Every university has certain standards that applicants must meet before being admitted. These standards usually include a high school diploma, a certain minimum score on standard achievement or admissions tests, evidence of financial ability to pay for school, a medical exam to determine the applicant's health, and personal references and/or recommendations from recognized authorities. Likewise, there were also admission standards in order for a piece of writing to be recognized as Spirit-inspired and admitted to the New Testament canon.

Apostleship

First, for a book to be canonized, it had to have been written by a true prophet or apostle or by someone in direct contact with them. The legitimacy and authenticity of this message was confirmed by accompanying supernatural acts of God (see Acts 2:22; 2 Cor. 12:12; Heb. 2:4). Matthew's, John's, and Peter's writings met that standard. Books like Mark, Luke, Acts, James, and Jude qualified because they were written by firsthand associates of the apostles, men who carried the apostles' stamp of approval. Paul's epistles bore the stamp of apostolic authorship because God called him to be the apostle to the Gentiles. We know that the books of Hebrews and 1, 2, and 3 John, which do not name the author, have apostolic authority because of the writing style and that they state that they were eyewitnesses of Jesus Christ.

Just as a contender for the New Testament had to meet the standard of apostolic authority, the standards were extremely high for inclusion in the Old Testament canon. The writer of Hebrews affirmed that God "spoke long ago to the fathers in the prophets in many portions and in many ways" (1:1). We get a glimpse of this in Exodus 24:3–4, which tells a story of Moses, the first prophet through which God spoke:

> Then Moses came and recounted to the people all the words of the LORD and all the ordinances; and all the people answered with one voice and said, "All the words which the LORD has spoken we will do!" Moses wrote down all the words of the LORD.

God spoke His revelation, and Moses wrote it down by inspiration. The reason we know God created the heavens and the earth is that God the Holy Spirit inspired Moses to record these events, even though no human being was present at creation. Moses did not just sit down, look up at the stars, and begin weaving stories about God. In fact, God established strict guidelines for His prophets that help us draw the line between true and false prophets even today. God said to Moses:

> I will raise up a prophet from among their countrymen like you, and I will put My words in his mouth, and he shall speak to them all that I command him. It shall come about that whoever will not listen to My words which he shall speak in My name, I Myself will require it of him. But the prophet who speaks a word presumptuously in My name which I have not commanded him to speak, or which he speaks in the name of other gods, that prophet shall die. (Deut. 18:18–20)

You can see why there wasn't a long line of people volunteering to be prophets in Old Testament days. If you tried to claim a true prophet's authority falsely, it would cost you your life. A prophet had a weighty responsibility because he had to speak the very words of God, just as he received them from God, and those words became the standard by which God's people would be judged. Thus, for a book to be recognized as canonical, it had to tell the truth *from* God and had to be true *about* God (Deut. 13:1–3).

By the time Moses was dead and Joshua had succeeded him as God's leader for Israel, Joshua had the writings of Moses to read and obey. That's why God commanded Joshua,

> This book of the law shall not depart from your mouth, but you shall meditate on it day and night, so that you may be careful to do according to all that is written in it; for then you will make your way prosperous, and then you will have success. (Josh. 1:8)

But then Joshua wrote the book that bears his name and added to the writings of Scripture. Joshua passed the test of being associated with a prophet. He was Moses's right-hand man. In the last chapter of Joshua, we are told: "And Joshua wrote these words in the book of the law of God; and he took a large stone and set it up there under the oak that was by the sanctuary of the LORD" (24:26). Joshua had the writings of Moses, but he also wrote under the Spirit's inspiration. The Bible accumulated over time as there developed a recognized chain of prophetic leaders whose writings were accepted as Scripture (2 Chron. 9:29). These men knew they were hearing from God (Jer. 1:2; Ezek. 3:1).

When it comes to the Old Testament canon, we have a witness to the authenticity of the books that goes back even before the beginning of the church. The Jews had recognized and brought together the books of the Hebrew canon many years before the days of Jesus and the apostles. In other words, God led the Jews to assemble their inspired canon—and the fact that God's people rejected a batch of other Jewish books, called the Apocrypha, is critically important, as we will see in a minute.

Each of the New Testament books, except Hebrews and 1, 2, and 3 John, carries the name either of an apostle or a personal associate of an apostle. Even Hebrews and 1, 2, and 3 John clearly demonstrate apostolic authority. And the apostles, particularly Paul, were not reluctant to claim God's inspiration for their writings.

For instance, Paul wrote, "For I would have you know, brethren, that the gospel which was preached by me is not according to man. For I neither received it from man, nor was I taught it, but I received it through a revelation of Jesus Christ" (Gal. 1:11–12). And again, "For this reason we also constantly thank God that when you received the word of God which you heard from us, you accepted it not as the word of men, but for what it really is, the word of God, which also performs its work in you who believe" (1 Thess. 2:13).

The apostles knew their writings were authoritative—and said so. But even Luke, who was not an apostle, was bold to say that he received the material for both volumes of his writings from the apostles (see Luke 1:1–4 and Acts 1:2).

And in a very important passage, Paul's writings received the apostolic seal of approval from Peter, who called Paul's letters "the Scriptures" (2 Peter 3:15–16).

Doctrinal Consistency

A second test of canonicity included whether the people of God recognized it as authoritative and accepted it as the Word of God. In other words, a book had to win a hearing from God's people as the Holy Spirit witnessed within them that the book's message was from God (see Neh. 8:9, 14–18; 1 Thess. 2:13) and stayed within the rules of faith previously established. As you recall, the term *canon* refers to a rule or authority, similar to a measurement standard. Irenaeus, a prominent early church leader (ca. AD 130–200), wrote about the church's discussion concerning maintaining this rule of faith (see Irenaeus, *Against Heresies*, Book 1, chapter 10), which was used to solidify consistency in teaching. This rule was a summary of what Christians had always believed, and it later became the basis for creeds such as the Apostle's Creed and the Nicene Creed.

The "rule of faith" operated as a guide for teachers and preachers in the church to make sure they stayed in line with the faith handed down through the apostles, what the epistle Jude calls "the faith which was once for all handed down to the saints" (v. 3). The rule of faith summarized God's work in creation, redemption (through the sending of His Son,

Jesus), and the consummation of His work in the final judgment. This same rule was used by church leaders (in conjunction with other things) to determine whether a written work should be considered part of the canon. Of course, this applied to the New Testament books only.

Internal Validation

We have seen that the Hebrew canon was already established by the time of Jesus. Our Lord quoted extensively from the Old Testament during His earthly ministry, and in so doing, validated the writings of the patriarchs and prophets (see Matt. 26:56; Luke 24:27). The appearance of Moses and Elijah with Jesus on the Mount of Transfiguration (see Matt. 17:3) was a powerful testimony of their authority as representatives of these two categories of Old Testament authors and also a powerful testimony that all of the Old Testament points to Jesus.

Notice how Paul also testified to the authority of the Old Testament and urged the church to make use of it in learning how God wants us to live. Paul wrote, "For whatever was written in earlier times [the Old Testament] was written for our instruction, so that through perseverance and the encouragement of the Scriptures we might have hope" (Rom. 15:4).

Elsewhere Paul said the events in the Old Testament "happened to them as an example, and they were written for our instruction" (1 Cor. 10:11). The New Testament quotes the Old Testament more than 250 times and alludes to it another nine hundred times. This is overwhelming evidence that the apostles—and Jesus—considered the Old Testament to be God's authoritative Word.

The Gospels came to the church bearing the stamp of inspiration, but they didn't come without some questions and debates. In fact, the entire canonicity of the New Testament was not as cut and dried as the Old Testament. With four gospel accounts as well as a wide variety of writers from various backgrounds, it took a bit longer for the ecumenical church to attain consensus on the canon of the New Testament.

The Synoptic Gospels (Matthew, Mark, and Luke) were among the first books of the New Testament to be widely recognized as part of the biblical canon. John's gospel took much longer to gain full recognition because it differed in more ways than Matthew, Mark, and Luke did from each other, and it made clearer claims about the divinity of Christ.

The New Testament epistles were used in and circulated among the churches, and they gained instant recognition as the Word of God. The teachings of the apostles were considered authoritative for the church (see 1 Cor. 14:37; 1 Thess. 2:4). The authors of these books often claimed inspiration for themselves (see Gal. 1:11–12; 1 Thess. 2:13). And the apostles' doctrines are consistent with one another—another key test of canonicity.

The canon of Scripture was not being fully settled until

about four hundred years after Christ. And even then, some books continued to be questioned by various leaders and councils, including 2 Peter, 2 and 3 John, James, Jude, Hebrews, and even Revelation.

Some people point to these historical facts as evidence that the process of assembling the canon was a subjective human work. Actually, they prove just the opposite. The fact that the canon of Scripture existed by informal recognition for so long shows the staying power of the books that God inspired. For instance, the gospel of Thomas had basically several hundred years to convince the church that it was from God, yet it did not make it into the canon because it is not Scripture. The lateness of the final canon is testimony to the fact that what the church had recognized and accepted all along as Scripture was valid.

Most of the doubts on these latter books had to do with the apostolic authorship of these books, but they proved their inspiration. Many of the doubts about James stemmed from a misunderstanding of James's teaching that we are saved by works and not by faith alone. Careful study and exposition of James has shown that those who thought James contradicted Paul's ringing declaration, "The righteous man shall live by faith" (Rom. 1:17), were simply wrong. James complements Paul by telling us that we authenticate our faith through our works.

The book of Revelation was the last book of Scripture

to be written and the end of the canon. It was questioned in part because its apocalyptic images seemed too fantastic to be real, but again, that doubt was settled by careful biblical interpretation.

John claimed that his message came straight from heaven (see Rev. 1:11), and he even added this curse to anyone who tries to add to or subtract from Scripture:

> I testify to everyone who hears the words of the prophecy of this book: if anyone adds to them, God will add to him the plagues which are written in this book; and if anyone takes away from the words of the book of this prophecy, God will take away his part from the tree of life and from the holy city, which are written in this book. (Rev. 22:18–19)

External Validation

While the actual date is unclear, it probably wasn't until the early part of the second century AD that the Christian church may have copied down, collected, and preserved every portion of the New Testament. Formal canonical lists were not established and widely circulated until the fourth and fifth centuries AD. By then, the argument over which books should be included had largely subsided, and final lists were drawn up at the synods of Hippo (AD 393) and Carthage (AD 397). Essentially, the church closed the canon of Scripture around this period. In doing so, they rejected heretical theologies. It is important to stand on the finality of the discernment of the ecumenical church, as this process was the result of surveying apostolic authorship and reception among those who lived closest to the time of Jesus Christ.

Now, let me touch on this briefly before we finish looking at the canon. Many Christians are aware that the Old Testament of the Roman Catholic Bible contains about a dozen extra books the Protestant church has rejected as noncanonical. They are called the Apocrypha, which means "secret things" or "secret writings."

One reason these books are in the Catholic Bible is that the Roman Catholic Church and Protestants take a fundamentally different approach to the issue of canonicity. The Catholic position is that the Church of Rome determines the canon. This means that even though the Hebrew canon does not contain the Apocrypha, and even though Jesus and the apostles never referred to them at all or quoted them, the Catholic Church believes it has the authority to declare these books as Scripture. (The Catholic Church canonized the Apocrypha at the Council of Trent in 1546.[3])

But the books of the Apocrypha fail on each criterion for

---

3. See Norman L. Geisler and William E. Nix, *A General Introduction to the Bible*, Revised, Expanded, Subsequent edition (Chicago: Moody Publishers, 1986), 274.

inclusion in the Bible. The fact that the Jews never accepted these books as part of the Old Testament is a hugely important witness against the Apocrypha as canonical. So is the silence of Jesus and the fact that the early church did not formally canonize the apocryphal books.

The apocryphal books also fail the test of internal evidence. They never claim to be the Word of God, and much of the content consists of the kind of "Jewish myths" that Paul warned the church to stay away from (Titus 1:14). In fact, 1 Maccabees 9:27 considers its time period as being characterized by an absence of prophetic witness. They also contain serious doctrinal errors such as teaching that we need to give money to go to heaven.

Part of the problem is that the Roman Church believes in apostolic succession: the view that the authority of the apostles was passed directly from the Twelve to the Roman Church, and is still in their hands. The Catholic Church is not alone in that view, by the way, for the Mormons also make the same claim. We know from the Bible that the era of the apostles ended when the last apostle died. How do we know? Because an apostle had to be an eyewitness of Jesus' resurrection (see Acts 1:22). Apostolic succession is not a biblical doctrine.

For a written work to be considered and included in the official canon of Scripture, it had to pass multiple standards of authorship, doctrinal consistency, internal testimony, and external validation. Through this unique, formalizing process, God has given us His truths in Scripture through the power of the Holy Spirit.

CHAPTER FOUR

TRANSMISSION

To help you appreciate the absolute necessity of Scripture, I want to explore four concepts that will enable you to accurately learn and teach God's Word. They include *revelation*, *inspiration*, *illumination*, and *reception*. We will look at the first three in this chapter and the fourth one in the next chapter. This will give greater room to the study of interpretation because it carries the greatest weight in arriving at how and what you preach as a pastor.

REVELATION

Revelation is like pulling back a curtain in order to see what's behind it. This involves divine disclosure, God unveiling information about Himself.

The reason revelation is critical is that we only get to know about God what He decides to reveal about Himself. God is utterly, totally different from you and me—so different that theologians call Him the "Wholly Other." We were made in His image, but He is distinct from His creation and separate from sin. Even to see Him is to die (Ex. 33:20), apart from Christ. God said through the prophet Isaiah,

> "My thoughts are not your thoughts, nor are your ways My ways," declares the LORD. "For as the heavens are higher than the earth, so are My ways higher than your ways and My thoughts than your thoughts." (55:8–9)

Instead of recognizing God as wholly different, people have always tried to create God in their own image. Whenever we try to adjust God to how *we* think or feel, we are left with something other than the God who reveals Himself. We also try to advise Him on how to be God. We have never been God. We have never created anything, but we want to advise God. However, God must reveal Himself if we are to know Him because He is higher than we are.

What is the nature of God's self-revelation in Scripture? We have one answer here in Isaiah 55. God's Word is that which "goes forth from [His] mouth" (v. 11). That is, God's revelation is intensely *personal*. It is intimately tied to who

He is. When you open your Bible, you are not just engaging in academic study. You are really trying to understand who God is. In the Scripture, God unveils Himself. When you look in the Word, you see God. And as we see in Hebrews 4:12–13, the Bible is not just an inanimate object. It is alive because it is the Word of the living God who reveals Himself in a personal way.

God's revelation is also *purposeful*. He says that when He sends forth His Word, "It will not return to Me empty, without accomplishing what I desire, and without succeeding in the matter for which I sent it" (Isa. 55:11). Moreover, "All Scripture is inspired by God and profitable" (2 Tim. 3:16). It acts; it does the things in our lives that God purposes shall be done. God doesn't lay His revelation out for us to look over and vote on. And He doesn't just toss words around with no purpose in mind. Every word that comes from God's mouth is infused with His purpose. And because God's Word is also infused with His life, it has the power to bring His purpose to pass. God's Word always produces the effect He intends.

A third characteristic of revelation is that it is *particular*. That is, the Bible is the complete Word of God for us, but it does not claim to be a total description of what God is like or a total record of everything God does. The last verse of John's gospel is important here. The apostle says that if all the things Jesus did were written down in detail, "even the world itself would not contain the books that would be written"

(John 21:25). Even if that statement is hyperbolic, it is still amazing. Remember, John is just talking about a brief slice of Jesus' earthly life, His three-year ministry. The Gospels just give us the highlights of Jesus' ministry, the selective details the Holy Spirit wants us to know.

Deuteronomy 29:29 says, "The secret things belong to the LORD our God, but the things revealed belong to us." What God has told us about Himself is what He wants us to know. But He has not told us everything because we could not comprehend it all.

The opening verse of Hebrews makes clear that the revelation of God is also *progressive*: "God, after He spoke long ago to the fathers in the prophets in many portions and in many ways, in these last days has spoken to us in His Son" (1:1–2a). The God who spoke through the prophets in the Old Testament spoke through Christ in the New Testament. God gave us His revelation one step at a time, not all at once.

INSPIRATION

While revelation is concerned with the content of Scripture, inspiration is concerned with the recording of that content. This word *inspire* has become watered down in our everyday usage. We say, "I was inspired by the choir." "The preacher inspired me." "That was an inspiring poem." We mean the person or piece made us feel good. It caused our spirit to be elevated.

That's a weak use of the word that does not properly express the biblical concept. We read above in 2 Timothy 3:16 that "all Scripture is inspired by God." The Greek word here, *theopneustos*, is made up of two words, the word for "God" and a word that means "to breathe out" or "exhale." All Scripture is the "exhaling" of God. He exhaled the Word upon the authors who recorded it.

When we talk about inspiration, we are talking about the process by which God oversaw the composition of Scripture so that its message was recorded without error. You may notice in your reading of Scripture that some translations of 2 Timothy 3:16 say "all" while others say "every." The Greek adjective *pas* can denote "every," putting the emphasis on "each and every Scripture," or it can mean "all," highlighting the unity of the Scripture itself.

The difference in emphasis on the individual parts (every) or the whole (all) does not change the meaning that the apostle Paul was conveying concerning Scripture. We can safely assert from this verse that the totality of Scripture, in its individual parts and in its whole, is in fact inspired by God. Significantly, when Paul writes that "All Scripture is inspired by God," he is referring to the biblical canon, which for him was the Old Testament. Since the New Testament had not been completed yet, the Old Testament was the apostle's "Scripture."

This helps to explain texts such as Acts 1:16, where Peter

is talking about the need to replace Judas among the apostles. He says, "Brethren, the Scripture had to be fulfilled, which the Holy Spirit foretold by the mouth of David concerning Judas, who became a guide to those who arrested Jesus." In verse 20, Peter went on to quote Psalm 69:25 and 109:8 and apply those texts to Judas.

The question is, "Who was speaking in the Psalms, the Holy Spirit or David?" David wrote the verse, but Peter said the Holy Spirit spoke it. Therefore, the Bible claims that what its human authors wrote is the same as the spoken Word of God.

How did this process give us a Bible that is free from error even though imperfect human beings were in the picture? We looked at this in the last chapter on the canonicity of Scripture, but let's review briefly here. The apostle Peter, who was one of those imperfect human beings, tells us how it happened:

> But know this first of all, that no prophecy of Scripture is a matter of one's own interpretation, for no prophecy was ever made by an act of human will, but men moved by the Holy Spirit spoke from God. (2 Peter 1:20–21)

The Greek word translated "moved" (*pheromenoi*) means to be "carried or driven along," like wind driving the sail of a ship. This word is used in Acts 27:15 to describe what happened when the ship that Paul was on got caught in a terrible storm and was eventually destroyed. "When the ship was caught in [the storm] and could not face the wind, we gave way to it and let ourselves be driven along."

Compare this with 2 Peter 1:21, and you get the picture of how divine inspiration worked. What the wind was to the sail of that ship, the Holy Spirit was to the writers of Scripture. They were moved by the Spirit where *He* wanted them to go, not where *they* wanted to go. They wrote what God wanted them to write.

To put it another way, the writers of Scripture were at the mercy of the Spirit. They didn't lose their personalities. Every biblical writer has his own style and vocabulary. But God expressed His perfect revelation through the various personalities of these "men moved by the Holy Spirit." The four gospels are a great example of God utilizing the personality, skills, and history of a human author to portray His Word. They record many of the same stories of Jesus, but we can see key differences in how the author's voice is used.

Just as the Holy Spirit protected Jesus, *the living Word*, from sin (see 2 Cor. 5:21), so He protected the Bible, *the written Word*, from error through His influence in the writing of Scripture. To suggest that there are errors in the written Word is to equally suggest there is sin in Jesus, since He testified to the validity of the written Word. The Spirit guarded the truth of God in a miraculous way so that what was written is what God said. John put it this way:

> If we receive the testimony of men, the testimony of God is greater; for the testimony of God is this, that He has testified concerning His Son. . . . And the testimony is this, that God has given us eternal life, and this life is in His Son. . . .
>
> These things I have written to you.
>
> (1 John 5:9, 11, 13a)

Notice that last phrase. The witness from God became a written revelation from God to His people. God the Holy Spirit inspired John to write what He wanted us to know in a language we could understand. Why? So we would have a permanent record of God's witness.

The result of inspiration is this: because of the overseeing and superintending work of the Spirit in the recording of Scripture, what you and I have is the inerrant, authoritative canon of Scripture. In the Bible, we have the authoritative revelation of God preserved in a written record. Those who reject the inspiration of Scripture have to do battle with Jesus Christ, because Jesus believed it was the Word of God. He said in Matthew 5,

"Do not think that I came to abolish the Law or the Prophets; I did not come to abolish but to fulfill. For truly I say to you, until heaven and earth pass away, not the smallest letter or stroke shall pass from the Law until all is accomplished." (vv. 17–18)

The "smallest letter or stroke" is the familiar "one jot or one tittle" (KJV). The smallest letter of the Hebrew alphabet is written like an apostrophe in English. A "stroke" is a tiny line that distinguishes one Hebrew letter from another. Jesus was saying, "God's Word is so true and authoritative that it will be fulfilled down to the most minute portion of a Hebrew letter." In fact, even after this universe is gone, God's Word will still be in effect. The result of inspiration is that the Word of God cannot possibly fail.

Proverbs 30:5–6 says, "Every word of God is tested. . . . Do not add to His words or He will reprove you, and you will be proved a liar." God doesn't need your or my help to get His message recorded. If He had wanted more written, He would have had more written.

In the Upper Room, Jesus prophesied that through the Holy Spirit, He would remind the apostles of everything they would need to know (John 14:26; 16:13). So, when they sat down to write Scripture, the Spirit saw to it that everything was written just as God willed it to be written.

Jesus said in John 10:35, "The Scripture cannot be broken." That means it's binding. No single part can be extracted from the whole. It's either all God's Word, or none of it is God's Word. Some people want to take out the parts of the Bible they don't like. But Jesus warned us, "Don't negate the Word of God for the traditions of men. Don't let what men have always done and believed stop you from doing what God says" (see Mark 7:8–9).

ILLUMINATION

The word *illumination* simply means enlightenment. It is the work of the Holy Spirit that allows us to understand, experience, and apply the truth of God to our lives.

Archimedes was a famous scientist in ancient Greece. It is said that after toiling over theory after theory and test after test, when Archimedes finally fine-tuned a process to identify the purity of gold, he cried out "*Eureka!*" (the Greek term meaning "I've found it"). As time went on, the term *eureka* was popularly associated with the excitement that comes when you finally understand something. *Eureka* describes the "lightbulb" moment when suddenly what was once shrouded in obscurity finally becomes clear.

The word *illumination* shares this same sense. It finds its root in the term *illume*, which means "to light up." If you've ever studied a foreign language, you may be able to recall when you finally understood what you read. People often speak of a moment when the language clicked for them, and they could operate with a deeper understanding of how the language worked. Yet in both examples of Archimedes and of language learning, there was a time of unknowing and darkness that preceded the *eureka* moment. In the same way, we all have experienced those moments when we do not understand what we are reading in the Bible.

Paul prayed in Ephesians 1:18 that "the eyes of your heart may be enlightened" so that the saints would understand the greatness of God's power and blessings available to them. First John 2:27 says that every Christian has what John calls "the anointing"—that is, the ability to receive, understand, and apply spiritual truth. There are no "super saints" when it comes to understanding Scripture. God wants every believer to be illuminated concerning His truth. The only catch is whether we are committed enough to seek it.

Before cable television came into my neighborhood, I used a television antenna. I had a workman come out one time because I was having problems with my reception. He said, "Your signal is strong, but your antenna is not pointed in the right direction."

The Word of God is strong. There's no problem with the signal. But our heart's antenna is often not pointed in the right direction. A lot of us are fiddling with our lives trying to fix them when the problem is that our spiritual antenna is not pointed toward God. Therefore, we cannot pick up the Spirit's signal.

But we all have the anointing within us, the illuminating work of the Spirit of God. That's why the psalmist wrote these verses in Psalm 119: "Open my eyes, that I may behold wonderful things from Your law" (v. 18). "Your commandments make me wiser than my enemies" (v. 98). "I have more insight than all my teachers" (v. 99). "Your word is a lamp to my feet and a light to my path" (v. 105).

The Spirit of God shines His light on the Word of God. Back in Genesis 1:2, we discover that the Spirit was hovering over creation. Then in verse 3 God said, "Let there be light." Light was not present until the Spirit of God hovered. Why is that important? When the Spirit of God hovers and the Word of God speaks, order comes out of chaos. That's what happened in creation. The earth was "formless and void" before the Spirit and the light came (Gen. 1:2).

Does your life ever feel formless and void? Does your life ever feel empty or chaotic? You move from chaos to order when the Spirit illuminates God's Word for you. That happens not when you simply read your Bible, but when you submit your heart to God's Word and ask His Spirit to move. Then God brings order out of chaos.

In 1 Corinthians 2, Paul makes some great statements concerning this matter:

Just as it is written, "Things which eye has not seen and ear has not heard, and which have not entered the heart of man, all that God has prepared for those who love Him." For to us God revealed them through the Spirit; for the Spirit searches all things, even the depths of God. . . . Now we have received, not the spirit of the world, but the Spirit who is from God, so that we may know the things freely given to us by God, which things we also speak, not in words taught by human wisdom, but in those taught by the Spirit, combining spiritual thoughts with spiritual words. (vv. 9–10, 12–13)

When the Spirit takes "spiritual words," the Word of God, and combines them with "spiritual thoughts," a mind and a heart in tune with God, the result is divine illumination. When you combine a spiritually receptive mind with the Word, you have dynamite on your hands. That's because "he who is spiritual appraises all things" (v. 15) since he has "the mind of Christ" (v. 16).

Luke 24:13–35, the story of the two disciples on the road to Emmaus, gives us a real-life look at how the process of illumination works. You'll remember that as these two walked back to Emmaus from Jerusalem, they were depressed, discouraged, and downcast. Life had fallen in for them because Jesus had been crucified. They saw "no hope, no way, no how."

But then the risen Christ joined them on the road and asked why they were discouraged (v. 17). They explained the situation and their disappointment, and Jesus said to them, "O foolish men and slow of heart to believe in all that the prophets have spoken!" (v. 25). Then He taught them from the Scriptures.

In other words, they had not been paying attention to the revealed Word of God. In effect, Jesus was saying, "You two are discouraged for no reason. If you would have listened to the Word of God, you would know that what has happened is a fulfillment of prophecy."

Because they weren't listening to the Word, they were unnecessarily depressed. But when Jesus began teaching them, they listened. If you want the illumination of the Spirit, the first thing you need is *a listening ear* to hear what the Word of God is saying (Rev. 2:11, 17, 29; 3:6, 13–22). Then you need to combine a listening ear with *the will to be transformed*. Verse 28 says that Jesus "acted as though He were going farther." But they begged Him, "Stay with us" (v. 29). I think Jesus was testing them to see whether they really wanted Him or were just going through the spiritual motions.

God does this with us. He will let us hear the Word, and then He will bring something into our lives to see whether we really heard it or whether we were just passively sitting in church or doing rote devotions that day. He will bring something into the lives of His people to put what they have heard or studied to the test.

So, we have a listening ear and a willing heart, two key elements in experiencing illumination. The third element is *worship*. Jesus reclined at the table with these two disciples, and they essentially worshiped (v. 30). In fact, we can see many of the same elements in verse 30 that we find later in Acts 2. There was communion in the breaking of bread, prayer, and *koinonia* (fellowship of believers) as Jesus shared the Word with them.

When all of that was working, what happened next? "Their eyes were opened" (Luke 24:31). Illumination occurred. They were enlightened. They recognized Him. Even though Jesus vanished from their sight in that instant, everything was changed. They were alive with joy and excitement, and they couldn't wait to share it with others. They got up, ran back to Jerusalem that same night, and excitedly told the apostles all that had happened to them (vv. 33–35).

It is important to note that illumination of the Word by the Spirit allows any believer to understand the Holy Scriptures. If you think about it, you hold in your hand sixty-six books written by and for kings and priests, but also written by and for shepherds and fishermen. God has the uncanny ability of wrapping up the profound in an accessible format. The Protestant reformers called this the "perspicuity of

Scripture," that the Bible could be understood through the guidance of the Spirit by king, clergy, and commoner alike. It is this principle that drove the heroic effort of Reformers like Martin Luther and William Tyndale in the sixteenth century to translate the Scriptures into the common language of their people, so that everyone would have the opportunity to read, study, and apply God's Word.

Tyndale famously quipped to a fellow minister, whose ignorance of Scripture was matched by his resistance to it being put in the hands of commoners, that "If God spare my life, ere many years pass, I will cause a boy that driveth the plow [to] know more of the Scripture than thou dost."[4] Essentially, Scripture is meant for everyone. Your primary job as a pastor or church leader is not only to further explain Scripture, but also to equip your people to study the Bible for themselves and apply it.

In revelation, God discloses His truth. Through inspiration, He sees that it is recorded for us. And by the illumination of His Spirit, He enables us to understand and apply it. When you get all of this working in your life, you're going to grow as a kingdom disciple.

---

4. "The Reformers," Lakemont Presbyterian Church (PCA) website, http://www.lakemont pca.org/the-reformers/.

CHAPTER FIVE

RECEPTION

---◆---

Once you've gone through the process of reading Scripture and interpreting it, the next step is to receive the Word into your own life. If the Word of God is not transforming you personally, then you will not be equipped to disciple others. So, before we get into the nuts and bolts of systematic exposition, let's first look at how the Word of God works in your own life.

SANCTIFICATION

As I mentioned earlier, when a person is born again, they receive a new nature by the animating power of the Holy Spirit (see 1 Peter 1:23). The new nature you receive continues to mature throughout your Christian life. Your old nature will fight against your new nature, even though you have the Spirit-life within you. In order for our soul—the very essence of who we are—to become what God wants it to become, to become conformed to Christ, the living Word of God, we must embrace the written Word of God.

What I'm about to share with you could be one of the most important principles you grasp as a pastor or leader, and in turn, teach to those under your care. With that in mind, consider what James writes: "This you know, my beloved brethren. But everyone must be quick to hear, slow to speak and slow to anger" (James 1:19).

James is talking to Christians. He calls them "beloved brethren." So these verses apply only to those who have trusted Christ for their salvation. James follows his introduction with a command that is part of the formula for preaching and teaching on true life transformation. He says *everyone* must be quick to hear, slow to speak, and slow to anger.

The question you might be asking is this: "Quick to hear *what*?" We will find out a few verses later in the passage that we are to be quick to hear God's point of view on a matter (see vv. 22–25). The other question you might be asking is this: "Slow to speak *what*?" We are to be slow to speak our point of view on a matter. And whenever the perspective of God's Word or of another person doesn't match our own, we should be slow to anger about it.

However, we often do the opposite. We are quick to

espouse our viewpoint on a matter and slow to hear others', especially God's point of view. But we should be quick to receive His point of view.

And why? James continues, "Therefore, putting aside all filthiness and all that remains of wickedness, in humility receive the word implanted, which is able to save your souls" (James 1:21).

First, James tells us to remove anything that will prevent us from receiving the word implanted." He then instructs us to "receive the word implanted, which is able to save [our] souls." This is where principles of interpretation and exposition come into play, because when you look at the context of the passage, you learn that the audience to whom he is writing is already saved. He just called them his beloved brethren. Yet he is also saying that their souls need to be saved. How can both be true?

When you and I trusted Christ for the forgiveness of our sins, our souls were saved eternally. But our souls were not saved, fully transformed, automatically in history.

When you trusted in Jesus for the forgiveness of sins, you brought your issues to the cross. You brought your past, your bondage, your propensities, and your problems to the cross. Jesus saved you for heaven in a flicker of time. But He saves you on earth progressively. First Corinthians 1:18 says that "the word of the cross is foolishness . . . but to us who are being saved" it is power. In that verse, we clearly see His reference to us as "being saved," or sanctified.

One of the reasons we are not experiencing total victory, even though we desire and promise to do better, is because the implanted Word has not been fully embraced. God says if you will ever receive what has been implanted within you, it will deliver your soul.

Only the Word of God, which quickens you by the power of the Holy Spirit, can bring you to maturity in Christ. Only God's Word and Spirit can sanctify your soul and conform all of who you are to the image of Christ.

But you say, "Wait a minute, Tony. I've studied my Bible for years. My soul has not changed. Or it changes for a while and then goes back to how it was before. Why isn't it working for me?" The answer is found in the word "receive." It is possible to have the Word implanted but to still have not received it. The word "receive" means more than just simply hearing, having, or knowing something. It means to "welcome" it. For example, when you welcome someone who is standing at the door of your home, you invite that person in. That person is now within your home. You didn't just stand at the door and say, "You are welcome." You ushered in that person, which enabled your "welcome" to be experienced and lived out.

When we "welcome" the Word of God, it goes to work in our souls. As we have referenced several times, in Hebrews 4:12, we learn that the Word of God is active and alive. The

Bible also calls the Word food for the soul. Just like you have food for the body that supplies proper nutrition to enable your body to function well, there is also food for the soul. Jesus said that man should not "live on bread alone, but on every word that proceeds out of the mouth of God" (Matt. 4:4). The book of Hebrews also tells us that when this food reaches the soul, it pierces as far as the division of our soul and spirit (see 4:12). But in order for it to do that, it needs to be received, welcomed.

God's Word is designed to bring about growth and transformation. The key, however, for the implanted Word to accomplish its life-giving work is the soil of the heart into which it is planted. How well that soil is able to receive the Word will impact how well it transforms one's life. Jesus makes this clear in His parable of the sower (Matt. 13:1–23; Luke 8:4–15). The effectiveness and productivity of the sower's work was not related to the seed but rather to the soil into which the seed fell. The soil is the condition of the heart of the one who hears God's Word.

If your heart is not good soil, then the Word cannot produce fruit and bring about transformation (Matt. 13:23). Just as bad soil will keep a good seed from accomplishing its goal, so an unresponsive and rebellious heart will keep God's Word from bringing sinners to salvation and Christians to maturity.

We must continually ask God to soften our hearts to His Word through worship, confession of sin, and the decision to seek to please Him in our choices. The more tender the heart becomes, the more powerfully the Word will do the work of sanctification in the soul of the believer.

Remember, your soul is your essence—your mind, emotions, and will. The writer of Hebrews says that the Word will judge the thoughts and intentions of the heart, the core of who you are. As the Word of God works on you, it will begin to dominate your thoughts, feelings, and will so that actions that reflect God's viewpoint will become natural for you.

INTIMACY WITH CHRIST

The Bible says the power of this transformative Word comes tied to a relationship. The power comes when the living Word, Jesus Christ, begins maturing our new nature, making us more like Him. This ongoing abiding with Jesus Christ allows our soul to be fed the spiritual nourishment of the Word of God. The Word is welcomed when we are pursuing a relationship with the Savior and not just information for a sermon or lesson. I'm ashamed to admit it, but in seminary I became more passionate about learning the Bible than I was about using it as the vehicle to grow closer to the Lord, a practice that Jesus clearly condemned (see John 5:39–40).

As our soul is fed, it is transformed. It is then that we find ourselves truly abiding in a power that is not our own. Our thoughts reflect His thoughts, our messages reflect His message, our views reflect His views, and our counsel reflects His counsel. When we receive the living words from Jesus Christ on an ongoing basis, His power manifests itself in our lives and ministries.

But the power of God's Word implanted within you is only manifested when you choose to abide with the living Word, Christ Himself. This is a critical aspect of receiving the Word of God for the purposes of life change and empowering your ministry. Abiding in Christ is another name for intimacy with Christ. Christ wants to express His life through you, which comes through your abiding in Him. Abiding means just what it says. It means to remain, to stay, to keep the connection strong. It's a freeing way to live because it means you can take a deep breath and just get to know Jesus. It takes away all the self-induced struggle.

The story is told that a bulldog and a poodle were arguing one day. The bulldog was making fun of the poodle, calling him a weak little runt who couldn't do anything.

Then the bulldog said, "I challenge you to a contest. Let's see who can open the back door of their house the fastest and get inside." The bulldog was thinking he would turn the doorknob with his powerful jaws and open the door, while the poodle was too small even to reach the knob on his back door.

But to the bulldog's surprise, the poodle said, "I can get inside my house faster than you can. I accept the challenge."

So with the poodle watching, the bulldog ran to the back

door of his house and jumped up to the doorknob. He got his teeth and paws around the knob and tried to turn it, but he couldn't get enough of a grip on the knob to turn it. He finally had to quit in exhaustion.

Now it was the poodle's turn at his back door. "Go ahead, you little runt," the bulldog growled, trying to soothe his wounded pride. The poodle went to the door and scratched a couple of times. The master not only opened the door, but lovingly picked the poodle up in his arms and carried him inside.

The difference was in the relationship. Some of us are bulldog pastors and church leaders. It's all grunting and growling and trying, when Christ wants us to come close to Him. There is a process to intimacy with Christ, and that is remaining in His Word.

He said, "If you abide in Me, and My words abide in you, ask whatever you wish, and it will be done for you" (John 15:7). He says that if we remain in Him and His words remain in us, then we can ask whatever we want and it will be done. We can ask for His blessing over our ministry, the expansion of our church, the health of our outreach and more and if these are God's will, He will grant them.

It is absolutely essential that you let God's Word be at home in you. Why? Because this is God's revealed will for you (John 8:31; 15:7). Abiding in the Word is not for super saints. It is what God expects from each of His children. We also need to abide in Him and His Word because of our still-sin-affected human nature. Embracing truth does not come naturally to us. We have to work at learning and living it because we were "by nature children of wrath" (Eph. 2:3), whose minds were in total rebellion against God.

PUT THE WORD INTO ACTION

But here's the question. How do I get His words to remain in me? How do I get His words to reach where God's Word has been planted? We need to look at James again to answer that. After we have received the Word, James tells us to be "doers of the word" instead of just "hearers." He explains why this is necessary in the following verses:

> For if anyone is a hearer of the word and not a doer, he is like a man who looks at his natural face in a mirror; for once he has looked at himself and gone away, he has immediately forgotten what kind of person he was. But one who looks intently at the perfect law, the law of liberty, and abides by it, not having become a forgetful hearer but an effectual doer, this man will be blessed in what he does. (James 1:23–25)

James says to "look intently" at the perfect law. He says to let the Word liberate you by not being a forgetful hearer of the Word but an effectual doer of the Word. In order to become an effectual doer of the Word, you must establish a relationship with the Word. A casual reading or study of the Word will never produce faithful doing.

In John 8:31, Jesus says that we are His disciples if we abide in His word. Think about an old corded telephone. It can function only when it is connected to the right wires, and when you disconnect the wires, the phone is useless.

When you abide with Jesus, His words, His perspective, His viewpoint on a matter transform your soul.

Here's how you'll know when your soul is being transformed and the Spirit is taking over. You'll know because the changes that take place inside of you will become natural to you. You won't have to force peace. You won't have to force joy. You won't have to force kindness to those people who really push your buttons.

This relationship and identification with Jesus Christ and His Word will let your soul know: *Hey, soul, that's not who we are anymore. We don't talk like that. We don't look at that. We don't treat people like that. We don't judge like that. We don't give up like that. We don't manipulate like that. That's not who we are now.*

REFLECT THE WORD

The last aspect I want to explore in this matter of applying Scripture to our lives is the need to reflect the Word. Let's explore the way in which this is done. James continues:

> If anyone thinks himself to be religious, and yet does not bridle his tongue but deceives his own heart, this man's religion is worthless. Pure and undefiled religion in the sight of our God and Father is this: to visit orphans and widows in their distress, and to keep oneself unstained by the world. (1:26–27)

The word "religion" as James uses it here has to do with our external spiritual activity, those things that other people can see and hear us doing and saying. James isn't saying that religious activity—or good works—saves us. Remember, he is talking to believers who have already been brought to life by the Word. But James is saying that genuine faith ought to produce genuine works.

It's interesting that James begins with the tongue, a subject he has a whole lot more to say about in chapter 3. No matter what we may be doing, if we cannot control that little appendage in our mouths, our religion is a waste of time. James says in 3:9 that we use the same mouth to bless God on Sunday and curse people on Monday. Then he asks a very good question: "Does a fountain send out from the same opening both fresh and bitter water?" (v. 11). The obvious answer is no. One proof that you have received the Word and are responding to it is the way you talk.

Our commitment to the Word of God will also be reflected in our works. James 1:27 talks about helping the helpless, those who can do nothing for us in return. So we're not looking at a business deal here. And we're not looking at those things which will make our church look good to the community, or bring in potential growth, or improve our social media status. When you are submitted to the Word, when the truth is getting down into your life, people who may otherwise not get noticed suddenly become very important to you. Serving and helping them becomes a necessity for you.

Following Christ will lead us to those who are poor and needy, both materially and spiritually. These are the kind of people Jesus sought and hung out with. If the Word is at work in you, it will reflect in what you do in your personal life and ministry.

Our commitment also reflects itself in our walk. The challenge here is "to keep [ourselves] unstained by the world." This is being in the world, but not of the world. We are supposed to mark the world for Christ, not allow the world to leave its mark on us. What happens when you spill something on your shirt, and the stain is really obvious? People say things like, "You must have spilled something on your shirt." They don't say things like, "That's a really nice shirt except for that little stain." Why don't people say that?

Because when you have a stain on your clothes, the stain attracts all the attention.

It's the same with our spiritual lives. When you allow the world to stain you by participating in its ways, the stain shows. How do you keep the stains of sin off you so you can reflect Christ to the world? You pray what David prayed at the end of Psalm 139: "Search me, O God, and know my heart; try me and know my anxious thoughts; and see if there be any hurtful way in me, and lead me in the everlasting way" (vv. 23–24).

In other words, the way you keep from letting the stain of sin spoil God's reflection in you is by opening your heart and life to His intense searching. How does God search us and know us? By the Spirit of God using the Word of God to dissect our hearts (Heb. 4:12).

We are cracked vessels, no doubt about it. We all have flaws. The only way to keep a leaky vessel full is to keep the faucet turned on. We have to keep the Word of God flowing through us, keeping us filled and clean. It's an absolute necessity. There's no other way to be a genuine, growing servant of Jesus Christ and true kingdom leader other than receiving the Word implanted and being personally transformed by it regularly. And one day, our cracks will be fully repaired, once we enter into God's fully established kingdom.

CHAPTER SIX

APPLICATION

◆

When the Word of God is applied in our lives as it is intended by God, it results in an abundance of personal growth. Personal application, which we discussed to an extent at the end of the last chapter, produces benefits in the lives of believers. It is critical that you understand this not only from a personally motivating standpoint but also so you can instruct your congregants as to why they should prioritize the study *and* application of God's Word.

GUIDANCE

One of the preeminent sanctifying benefits of applying Scripture is that it gives us sound direction for all of life. Our need for God's guidance is nothing new. Throughout the Bible, God's people cry out for His help when they either reach a fork in the road or have their backs against the wall. Moses and the Israelites are trapped between the Red Sea and the Egyptian army in Exodus 14 when God tells them to move forward into the sea. Solomon prays as he assumes the throne of Israel, "I am but a little child; I do not know how to go out or come in" (1 Kings 3:7). Solomon then asks for wisdom to guide God's people.

I'm sure you know what it feels like to be in a major dilemma. You encounter situations in which you simply don't know which way to go. At times like this, you need a light to guide you, which makes the psalmist's ancient statement of God's guidance wholly relevant for us today: "Your word is a lamp to my feet and a light to my path" (Ps. 119:105). The Bible shows us the direction we should take. We do not have to wander aimlessly in the fog of human opinion.

One of the truths in this great verse that stands out is how personal and specific the guidance is that we receive from God's Word. We can see this, for instance, in the psalmist's use of the word *lamp*. Lamps in biblical days were a far cry from the kind of lighting we have today. Our lights can illuminate an entire room or a large area. And if we are walking in the dark, we have flashlights that can brighten up the path and show us any hidden obstacles. But in biblical days, a small oil lamp was a personal item, providing only enough light for a person to see the next step as he walked.

So a person had to walk carefully, watching each step. This is true of so many decisions and choices in life. Rarely if ever do we see an entire issue in one grand moment of illumination and know instantly everything to do. God has designed life in such a way that we have to trust Him one step at a time. His Word gives us light for the next step.

The first-person pronouns of Psalm 119:105 also reveal that this issue of guidance is personal. It's amazing how one Christian can open the Word and find clear guidance, while another can read the same passage and see nothing. This is true even though believers read the same Bible and have the same Holy Spirit. He reveals Himself to those who seek Him with all their hearts (see Jer. 29:13). Two Christians can be very different in their sensitivity to the Spirit and His ministry of illuminating the Word.

BLESSING

Psalm 1:1–3 is a guide for blessing that is both timeless and rich. It doesn't contain any tips on how to get ahead in the stock market or how to land that dream job. What it offers is infinitely better—a pattern for spiritual living that pleases God and opens the treasure stores of heaven.

> Blessed is the man
>   who walks not in the counsel of the wicked,

nor stands in the way of sinners,
    nor sits in the seat of scoffers;
but his delight is in the law of the LORD,
    and on his law he meditates day and night.

He is like a tree
    planted by streams of water
that yields its fruit in its season,
    and its leaf does not wither.
In all that he does, he prospers. (ESV)

It isn't immediately evident in English translations, but "blessed" in verse 1 is a plural Hebrew word that could be translated, "How many are the blessednesses of . . ." That may not be very smooth English, but it's great theology! When you seek God, you get blessings multiplied, an abundance of blessings.

The Hebrew verb "to be blessed" basically means "to be happy." We all want to be happy, and God wants us to be happy too—and in ways we can't even imagine. It's just that our concept of happiness does not always match His. Biblical happiness is neither the carefree, sail-through-life happiness nor the "name it, claim it" theology that says God's greatest desire for you is that you be healthy and wealthy. What does it mean, then, to be blessed in the biblical sense? Here is a simple definition: *a blessing is the God-given capacity to enjoy and extend the goodness of God in your life.*

Many people would look at this definition and think it misses the mark. They believe the blessing is the *thing itself* that God has given you out of His goodness, not the *capacity to enjoy and extend* God's goodness. Here are five questions you can ask yourself to determine whether you have a healthy view of biblical blessedness.

Do I Have Peace?

According to Proverbs 10:22, "It is the blessing of the LORD that makes rich, and He adds no sorrow to it." So if you're getting what you want—or working hard to get it—but all you have to show for it are headaches, sleepless nights, and a load of grief, then what you have or what you want may not be a blessing from God.

How do you know whether you're on the right track? One way to discern this is to compare your pursuit with the weary working man of Ecclesiastes 4:8. This guy doesn't even have any dependents to worry about, and yet the Bible says he was working himself to death. "There was no end to all his labor," "his eyes were not satisfied with riches," he was "depriving [him]self of pleasure," and it was all "a grievous task." You don't have to shred your soul to enjoy God's blessing.

Am I Content?

Paul says, "If we have food and covering, with these we shall be content" (1 Tim. 6:8). Now don't misread that. Paul isn't saying we have to live in a monastery cell and consume only bread and water. He experienced times in his ministry when he could afford a steak dinner, so to speak (Phil. 4:11–12, discussed later). But Paul also knew what it was to have nothing. His point is that once we become discontent with what God provides and "want to get rich" (1 Tim. 6:9), we lose the focus God wants us to have, which is to "pursue righteousness, godliness, faith, love, perseverance and gentleness" (v. 11).

The Bible is clear that happiness does not depend upon our financial, emotional, or physical circumstances. And yet, God's Word says He wants every one of His children to be blessed. That's why I like the definition of blessedness as the God-given capacity to enjoy and extend His goodness. This definition provides the common denominator that allows any Christian in any age and in any circumstance to be a full-fledged candidate for God's blessing. Paul addressed this in Philippians 4:11–12:

> Not that I speak from want, for I have learned to be content in whatever circumstances I am. I know how to get along with humble means, and I also know how to live in prosperity; in any and every circumstance I have learned the secret of being filled and

going hungry, both of having abundance and suffering need.

Paul's secret to contentment, or happiness, is his focus on Christ "in any and every circumstance."

Whose Counsel Do I Follow?

The false views of happiness are typical of the kind of "counsel" or advice that the world offers us, and that Psalm 1:1 warns us to avoid: "Blessed is the man who walks not in the counsel of the wicked, nor stands in the way of sinners, nor sits in the seat of scoffers" (ESV).

The "wicked" are not just terribly evil people, but those who do not take God and His Word into account. We are not to "walk," or conduct our lives, according to the perspective of people who have a man-centered, instead of a God-centered, worldview. If you want to enjoy God's goodness, don't go to folk who have no regard for God in order to get advice on how to live. A lot of us aren't enjoying and extending the goodness of God because we're receiving counsel from the wrong people.

God's blessings are also not found in "the way of sinners." When the psalmist talks about standing, he means where you hang out and who your friends are. The people you stand with are those you identify with and those who have an influence on you. The Bible says a person who wants God's blessing will not hang out in the company of people who disregard God's law and make a habit of breaking it.

There is a third place you want to avoid if you are seeking God's blessing (enjoying and extending the goodness of God). The last part of Psalm 1:1 says that the blessed person does not sit "in the seat of scoffers." A scoffer is someone who makes light of serious things. To scoff is to express contempt or mockery that isn't deserved. The word *seat* suggests someone who sits in judgment. In Old Testament days, the elders of a city sat at the city gate to conduct business and also to hear cases and render judgments. Thus, a scoffer sets himself up as judge and jury in matters he doesn't even understand. Scoffers are people you don't want to be influenced by.

Did you notice the progression in verse 1? The not-blessed person, if we can use that term, starts off walking by the wrong crowd and stopping to ask for advice. Then he decides to hang with this crowd, and finally he becomes so comfortable with them that he sits down with them. This is a warning for all of us, because we all have had times when we went from feeling uncomfortable in the wrong situation to tolerating it and then, finally, feeling at home with it. If we're not careful, this can become a lifestyle, and when that happens, we forfeit God's blessings.

Am I Delighting in and Meditating on God's Word?

Now that we know that the path to blessedness is not

found in following the world, we can look at where God's blessing can be found. The psalmist answered this with a clear declaration that God's blessings are inextricably tied to His Word: "But his delight is in the law of the LORD, and in His law he meditates day and night" (Ps. 1:2).

The word "delight" refers to the enjoyment of and pleasure in something or someone. When you delight in someone, you want to be with that person all the time—and when you're not together, you can't stop thinking about that person. When you delight in a song, you play or hum the tune again and again.

The writer of Psalm 1 says that the blessed or happy person delights in God's Word and allows it to occupy his mind. You may say, "I've got a family and a job. I can't sit around all day reading the Bible." That's true, but this is not what the verse is about. The key is in the word "meditate."

For instance, did you know that persistent worry is a negative form of meditation? When you are worried about something, you can't get it out of your mind no matter what you are doing. People spend a lot of time "meditating" on their financial situation. Some people meditate on their favorite television program or sports team. What we meditate on, what we think about the most and what consumes our affections, comes out in what we talk about the most.

So let's not use the "I don't know how to meditate" excuse as a reason for not focusing our minds on God and His Word.

We all meditate. It's simply a matter of what we are meditating on. So, we need to think about what our lives would look like if we systematically and seriously applied the Scripture we are dealing with.

One way to meditate on the Word is to roll it over and over in your mind and ask, "God, how does Your Word affect what I'm facing right now? What does it say about my response to what I'm facing? How can Your Word change what I'm thinking and feeling right now if my attitude is not right? How does Your Word equip me to deal with the things I am facing?" Meditation connects God's Word to life's realities. The difference between hearing God's Word and being blessed by it is called meditation.

Why does God want us to meditate on His Word? There are many reasons, including the need to avoid sin (see Ps. 119:11). The Bible is the repository of our spiritual blessings. Psalm 1:3 says of the blessed person, "He will be like a tree firmly planted by streams of water, which yields its fruit in its season and its leaf does not wither; and in whatever he does, he prospers." A tree is a great word picture of someone who is enjoying God's goodness and blessings in spite of circumstances. The Bible uses grass to illustrate something that is transitory (see Isa. 40:7–8 and Matt. 6:30). But a tree illustrates that which is meant to last.

The psalmist continued to describe the blessed person as a tree "firmly planted." This is a picture of stability, being firmly anchored. I can get a tall ladder, lean it against a building, then climb to the top of the ladder and stand there. But there is a fundamental, all-important difference between me on a ladder and a tree. Unless Superman is holding that ladder for me, I am not firmly planted. The next puff of wind could blow me over.

When you are firmly planted, the stuff that used to blow you over doesn't knock you down anymore. You may bend in the wind, but your root system will hold you if your roots are planted deeply in God's Word. The writer of Hebrews called our hope in Christ "an anchor of the soul" (6:19). Guess where we learn about that hope? In God's revealed Word.

Notice also that the leaf of the blessed person "does not wither." This tree is an evergreen, in other words. There is a freshness and vibrancy about a person who is being blessed by God. It doesn't mean we never feel sad or burdened, or experience anguish. The Bible doesn't say the leaves won't shake in the wind sometimes. Those are the external circumstances we can't control. But the leaves of our lives won't die and fall off from the internal lack of water when we are tapped into God and His Word. The person who knows and lives in God's Word enjoys a continuous source of life.

Am I Producing Good Fruit?

The middle of Psalm 1:3 says a blessed person "yields" or produces fruit. This refers to taking that internal nourishment and refreshment and turning it into something that other people around you can enjoy too. If you're being blessed but all you are passing on to others is a sour, dried-up piece of fruit, your blessing is stopping at the wrong station. Fruit always reflects the character of the tree it comes from.

Your capacity to enjoy God should give you something to share. A tree doesn't yield fruit for its own consumption. But fruit always exists for the benefit of another. So, one way you know you're blessed is that you are being a blessing.

Now, look at the summary statement of this great passage. Whatever the blessed person does "prospers." God can make such a great promise because the person who is delighting in and meditating on His Word will reflect God's mind and heart. God's blessing will prosper you, in that you will know His pleasure on your life.

That's quite a package of blessing. There is no question about God's desire to deliver His blessing. The only question is whether we are putting ourselves in a position to receive and enjoy His goodness and then extend it to others.

FREEDOM

We are new creations now in Christ, but we are still sinful—which you realize when you try to do the right thing and wind up doing the wrong thing. As the bumper sticker says, "Christians aren't perfect, just forgiven." At least we're in good company, because in Romans 6–7, the apostle Paul wrestles with the question, "If I'm a Christian, why am I doing the very things I don't want to do?" His answer clarifies that it was "the law of sin which is in my members [of his body]" (Rom. 7:23).

Keep on reading, though, because Paul isn't making excuses for himself—or for us. Here is his conclusion to the matter: "Thanks be to God through Jesus Christ our Lord!" (v. 25). Why? Because "the law of the Spirit of life in Christ Jesus *has set [me] free* from the law of sin and of death" (Rom. 8:2, emphasis added). This is the Christian's "emancipation proclamation."

But Paul also tells the Galatians, "It was for freedom that Christ set us free; therefore keep standing firm and do not be subject again to a yoke of slavery" (5:1). How can someone who has been set free by Jesus Christ be in danger of becoming a slave again? We can rule out the loss of salvation, because that can never happen to true believers (John 10:28). Salvation was not the issue in Galatians 5, but whether these Christians would allow themselves to be subjected to the demands of the Mosaic Law instead of living by grace. One of the ironies of the Christian life is that the Bible tells us to be who we already are. God says we need to behave like His children because that's who we are. And we are told to make sure we live in the freedom that Christ purchased for us because we are, in fact, free people.

We are abiding in Christ, and His Word is abiding in us, when we are enjoying His company through the Word. When the Bible becomes that precious to us, we will begin to experience what Jesus meant when He said, "If the Son makes you free, you will be free indeed" (John 8:36). "Indeed" means "sure enough" or "certainly." It means this is the real deal, because the Son has the authority to set us free and keep us free.

VICTORY

God's Word also has an announcement for the devil. In the words of David to Goliath, "The battle is the LORD's and He will give you into our hands" (1 Sam. 17:47). The enemy Goliath, who stood for all that was evil, was a terrifying presence with his huge size, heavy armor, and gigantic weapons. But like our enemy Satan (see 1 Peter 5:8), Goliath was a toothless lion because David was fighting in the Lord's name and strength. In the end, it was no contest. David's little stones and sling, not Goliath's huge spear, were the mighty weapons because this was not really a battle of the flesh but of the spirit.

The psalmist proclaimed, "O sing to the LORD a new song, for He has done wonderful things, His right hand and His holy arm have gained the victory for Him" (Ps. 98:1). This is the victory we want as Christians, what the apostle John called "the victory that has overcome the world—our faith" (1 John 5:4).

Now, if we are talking about achieving victory, and the context of that victory is spiritual warfare, then we need the right weapons to fight with. This is where the Bible comes in, for it not only tells us about the weapons God has given us, but it *is* our primary weapon for defeating Satan and laying claim to spiritual victory.

The reason the Bible is the Spirit's sword instead of an actual steel blade is that "our struggle is not against flesh and blood, but against the rulers, against the powers, against the world forces of this darkness, against the spiritual forces of wickedness in the heavenly places" (Eph. 6:12; see also 2 Cor. 10:3–4). If you're fighting with other people because you think they are the enemies keeping you from enjoying the victory God promises to His people, you are on the wrong battlefield.

Ephesians 6 makes it crystal clear that when it comes to spiritual warfare and the issue of our victory, the matter has already been settled. How do we know? Well, if you read the spiritual warfare passage in Ephesians 6:10–17, you will notice that nowhere are we told to attack the enemy and try to overcome him. Instead, our job is to "stand firm" (v. 11; see also vv. 13–14).

Now why would a soldier be told to stand firm instead of to attack and advance? Because he already has the territory his commander wants to take, and his job is to hold on to it. Jesus Christ defeated the devil and all of his army on the cross, and nothing can cancel out that victory. The result is that we are not fighting for victory, but from a position of victory. Satan is a defeated foe.

The sword of the Spirit, the Word of God, is the only offensive weapon in our Christian armory. Paul likened it to a particular kind of sword that Roman soldiers carried, one that all his readers in Ephesus would have been familiar with: "the sword of the Spirit, which is the word of God" (Eph. 6:17). The sword mentioned here is not the long sword we usually see in the old movies hung at a soldier's side in a sheath. The word for "sword" here refers to a much shorter, dagger-like weapon that a soldier carried in his belt for quick access in case he got into close combat. A soldier sometimes used both hands to wield his long sword. But his short, dagger-like sword could be applied much more directly and with a deadly result.

I'm making this point in depth because this is the word that Paul chose under the Holy Spirit's inspiration to describe what God's Word is designed to do for us in spiritual battle. It's important to understand that spiritual warfare is not swinging at the enemy from a distance, but close combat. The devil may be beaten, but he is still alive and well for now, and he loves nothing better than to get in your face and kick sand in it. That's why victory in spiritual warfare requires a weapon that can deliver precise blows.

Another Greek word in Ephesians 6:17 is very enlightening as we seek to understand how to win at spiritual warfare.

Paul called the Spirit's dagger "the word of God"—but we need to pause here, because this is not the ordinary word for Scripture. Paul did not use the familiar Greek word *logos*, which looks at the Bible in its entirety as the received body of God's truth.

Instead, Paul used the word *rhema*, which means "an utterance," and looks at the Bible not just as a bound volume of sixty-six books, but also as a weapon ready at hand to be used in a definite way in a definite time of need. Paul was saying that if we want to be victorious in spiritual warfare, we must be able to draw on specific truths from the Bible in specific situations to counter specific temptations and attacks from the enemy. You can have the entire *logos* of God on your shelf, the very Word of God that is complete and true in every syllable, and yet not be well-armed for spiritual warfare because you don't know how to draw on the *rhema* of God when you are under attack.

Until the *logos* of God also becomes the *rhema* in your hand to defeat the enemy, you won't see the Bible's power at work. As long as the Bible is just a bunch of general statements to you, you'll get general results. But someone who is filled and controlled by the Holy Spirit, and who knows how to handle the sword of the Spirit in specific spiritual encounters, can win any battle.

Now don't misunderstand me. I'm not saying that the Bible becomes sharp and powerful only when we start using it properly. In fact, one of the foundational verses of this entire study says exactly the opposite. "The word [*logos*] of God is living and active and sharper than any two-edged sword" (Heb. 4:12). Guess what word for "sword" the writer used here? You got it—the Roman short sword/dagger we've been talking about. So here is a text that joins the *logos*, all of God's Word, with this concept of a sharp, precision weapon, just as Ephesians 6:17 does with *rhema*. God's Word is sharp regardless of whether we ever discover that reality for ourselves.

The reason you want to learn the Bible generally is so you can use it specifically when the need for victory in spiritual warfare arises. I want to be victorious in my Christian life, not just barely hang on until I die or Jesus returns with angelic reinforcements. The great thing about the *rhema* of the Spirit is that it can keep you out of unnecessary battles as well as give you power to use in aggressive spiritual warfare.

Would you like to have Satan leave you alone for a while and have angels minister to you? Then use God's Word to send him packing like Jesus did in the desert. Satan cannot stand the Word of God. He isn't afraid of you or your words, but the sword of the Spirit will cut him up so badly he can't take it anymore.

You may be wondering what role angels play as regards your victory. Don't worry, they're out there. God has a spiritual support system waiting to go into action that can do powerful things beyond your wildest ability to conceive of (see Eph. 3:20–21—and sharpen your sword, the *rhema*, by memorizing it!). But if Matthew 4 teaches us anything, it teaches us that God's power is released by our willingness to use His Word verbally and defeat the devil in real combat.

THE TRUE GOD, THE PASTOR, AND THE LAW

The heart of the myriad of problems and issues facing us as a nation—in our communities and churches—fundamentally rests on an absence of three things: a correct understanding of God, pastors who accurately administer the Bible, and God's law. A somewhat obscure, yet entirely profound, passage in 2 Chronicles 15 outlines this for us. While this passage records specific circumstances thousands of years ago, in many ways it reflects our current situation. It highlights the lack of proper administration of a kingdom theology as the cause for societal, familial, and individual breakdown:

> "For many days Israel was without the true God and without a teaching priest and without law. . . . In those times there was no peace to him who went out or to him who came in, for many disturbances afflicted all the inhabitants of the lands. Nation was crushed by nation, and city by city, for God troubled them with every kind of distress." (vv. 3, 5–6)

This is a picture of great spiritual and social chaos, the breakdown of a society. So what was wrong? Three crucial ingredients, if you will, were missing in the administration of Israel's national life, and I believe they are missing today in our nation and in our churches. If you are a pastor or church leader, you have been positioned to stand in the gap for such a time as this.

The first missing ingredient was "the true God." Now the chronicler was not saying that the Israelites had become atheists or no longer believed in God. He wasn't saying that attendance at the temple was down. The sacrificial fires at the temple were still going. But Israel had lost a correct view of God, and the nation was no longer accomplishing His agenda.

The Israelites wanted a convenient God, one they could control. Essentially, they wanted a kingdom without a King. They wanted a mere figurehead, a puppet with but the trappings of kingship only. Yet if you have a God you can control, then you are god instead of Him. The Israelites didn't want the true God interfering with their national life, reminding them that He had an agenda greater than their personal interests and desires. Our culture doesn't want a God like that either. Our culture wants to pay homage only—to offer a nice, little prayer before public meetings—but we don't want to hear from the true God. The true God does not adjust to you. You adjust to Him.

Any time we simply pay homage without submitting our thoughts and actions under God's revealed Word, we are reinforcing our culture's false view of God as a harmless deity who doesn't have anything significant to say about the educational, scientific, entertainment, civic, political, familial, legal, or racial issues of the day. In doing so, we leave God the title of King in name only, but give His direction and authority to others, or even ourselves.

The second ingredient missing in Israel was a lack of teaching priests. Today, that could be translated to mean a lack of pastors preaching in biblical exposition. Again, the text doesn't say there were no priests. But the priests had stopped teaching the Word of God. They had traded divine revelation for entertainment or ritualism. Worship had degenerated into a social gathering. The temple no longer served as the epicenter of all life and conscience of the culture, calling people to take God seriously and reminding them of what His Word said. No real discipleship was occurring.

Israel was suffering from an absence of spiritual leaders who took seriously the authority of Scripture for all of life. Too often today, pastors preach to please and fear that someone might say, "Well, I didn't like that sermon," and then take their membership elsewhere. But if congregants say that when the pastor lovingly and passionately preaches God's Word, then they have given a wrong response. And if pastors cater to these sort of responses and thus preach to please, then they too are out of line. The issue is whether the message is true, not whether it is popular.

The third missing ingredient in Israel was God's law, or God's Word. There's only one standard of truth: the changeless Word of the one, true God. But once God's law is removed from or marginalized in a culture, then the standard for a society is gone, and God becomes one's worst enemy. That's what had happened in Israel. When God's law was missing, chaos reigned. You cannot have order and structure in society without God's truth.

The issue of truth is all-important, as we've seen in our time together in this book. The lack of truth leads to a "conscienceless" society. People become anesthetized in their conscience, losing their sense of right and wrong, and the Word of God is not there to convict people of sin. In such a society, every person becomes a law unto himself or herself, so chaos rules and truth loses meaning.

The stunning thing about the situation in 2 Chronicles 15 is that God caused Israel's distress; neither sinners in that culture nor Satan caused it. Now when God is your problem, then only God is your solution. If God is upset, it doesn't matter whom you elect or what programs you initiate. When God leaves a society, hope goes with Him and the society deteriorates. But as long as you have God, you always have hope.

The net result of these three missing ingredients in our world is that we are seeing the "devolution" of mankind.

The more we marginalize God, the worse things get. This is what Paul is getting at in Romans 1:18, where he writes, "The wrath of God is revealed from heaven against all ungodliness and unrighteousness of men." Then in verses 19–31, Paul traces the downward spiral of a culture that excludes God. This downward spiral *is* the passive wrath of God when He gives mankind the independence from Him that they desire.

What must we do to reverse this downward spiral? It is time to return to the King, His rules, and His kingdom agenda, the visible manifestation of the comprehensive rule of God over every area of life. What He says transcends human politics, secular social movements, and religious traditions. Until we as pastors and church leaders teach the Scripture from the vantage point of the kingdom thread woven within it, our congregants will not be equipped to fully submit themselves to the Lord as King.

Your job as a pastor and church leader is to administrate the application of the kingdom worldview through teaching, counseling, and preaching from the Scripture, utilizing the Word to its fullest and emphasizing how the kingdom connects throughout. It is time to recognize that the kingdom of God is not an ethereal fairy tale located in some far-off land. It is both here and now.

May it be said of us, when only our legacy is left, that we administered the responsibilities given to us as leaders under God to influence and impact the realms He has given us for good in His kingdom. Scripture has provided us with a clear authority and a comprehensive, dynamic approach to all of life. When the Word of God is applied and taught so that our lives are lived out in proper relationship to our King, His kingdom, and to each other, God will enable us, our families, and our churches to thrive according to the riches of His glory. Only when Israel returned to God did the situation in their culture improve (2 Chron. 15:4). God is waiting on you to return to Him through His Word and encourage others to do the same so He can work through His church to influence the culture (Matt. 16:18–19).

APPENDIX A

---◆---

RECOMMENDED RESOURCES

STUDY BIBLES

Tony Evans Study Bible

Ryrie Study Bible

MacArthur Study Bible

Jeremiah Study Bible

CONCORDANCES AND PARALLEL REFERENCE WORKS

These resources include alphabetical listings of words (or topics) in the Bible, showing the biblical references where each occurs. This is a must in locating passages and in studying topics.

Young's Analytical Concordance of the Bible

> Keyed to the KJV, its great strength is the analysis done which allows you to find every place a particular Greek or Hebrew word is located. Get the one by Eerdmans.

Strong's Concordance

> Its great strength is the numbering system, which is tied in with many other study tools.

New American Standard Exhaustive Concordance

> The only exhaustive concordance based on the New American Standard Bible. Every word in the NASB is listed (except words like "and," "the," etc.). References use the same numbering system as *Strong's Concordance*, thus making other word study tools accessible. It includes Hebrew and Greek dictionaries.

NIV Concordance

> An excellent concordance, but only for the NIV Bible.

Treasury of Scripture Knowledge

> This includes chronological data, concise chapter introductions, key word listings, illustrative notes, and over 500,000 Scripture references and parallel passages.

Nave's Topical Bible

> Nave's is the best known and most comprehensive of the topical Bibles, containing over 20,000 topics and subtopics and 100,000 Scripture references.

BIBLE DICTIONARIES AND ENCYCLOPEDIAS

These are alphabetical listings of people, places, things, events, and topics in Scripture. They contain definitions, historical and cultural background material, outlines, and more.

New Bible Dictionary

This is the best one-volume Bible dictionary available today. Maps, diagrams, and charts expand and clarify the text.

Zondervan Pictorial Encyclopedia of the Bible

This excellent five-volume work covers in a well-rounded way significant issues relating to doctrines, themes, and biblical interpretation.

Unger's Bible Dictionary

With its 1,200 pages and 7,000 articles, *Unger's Bible Dictionary* has proved its value as an authoritative reference work, encyclopedic in its scope.

New International Standard Bible Encyclopedia, revised

This new edition, in four volumes, by G. W. Bromiley is fully revised, and the articles retained from the original edition have been completely updated (many completely rewritten) to take into account recent discoveries in archaeology and advances in other areas of biblical scholarship.

ONE VOLUME BIBLE COMMENTARIES

These are verse-by-verse explanations and interpretations of the Bible. They are necessarily brief.

Tony Evans Bible Commentary

The Bible Knowledge Commentary, Old Testament and *The Bible Knowledge Commentary, New Testament*
>   These helpful volumes are written by the Dallas Theological Seminary faculty.

Wycliffe Bible Commentary

The New Bible Commentary, revised
>   Thoroughly revised and updated, this work provides good exposition that is often difficult to find in a one-volume commentary.

Moody Bible Commentary

MacArthur Bible Commentary

MULTIVOLUME BIBLE COMMENTARIES

The Expositor's Bible Commentary
>   This series of volumes, based on the NIV, provides pastors and other Bible students with a comprehensive and scholarly tool for the exposition of the Scriptures and the teaching and proclamation of their message.

Tyndale Old Testament and New Testament Commentaries
This series does much of the same that the Expositor's Bible Commentary does.

The Wiersbe Bible Commentary

The Grace New Testament Commentary

BIBLE DOCTRINE

These resources provide systematic presentations of biblical truth about God, the Bible, Jesus, the Holy Spirit, man, salvation, the church, and the future.

Theology You Can Count On

A Survey of Bible Doctrine

Major Bible Themes

Basic Theology: A Popular Systematic Guide to Understanding Biblical Truth

Moody Handbook of Theology

The Grace Soteriology, revised

Final Destiny: The Future Reign of the Servant Kings

The Kingdom Agenda: Living Life God's Way

BIBLE HANDBOOKS

These are gold mines of all kinds of helpful information about the Bible and related subjects such as archaeology, geography, history, as well as notes and outlines of the Bible itself.

The New Unger's Bible Handbook

What the Bible Is All About

BIBLE SURVEYS

These surveys provide historical, geographical, political, and archaeological background as well as outlines for each book. They also cover the origin, date and place of writing, content, outline, emphasis, characters, and special features of each book of the Bible.

A Popular Survey of the Old Testament

New Testament Survey, revised

BIBLE ATLASES

These include maps of Bible lands, showing where the various events took place and giving helpful background information.

Moody Atlas of the Bible

This resource is new, conservative, and extremely helpful.

The Macmillan Bible Atlas

This is produced by excellent cartographers (mapmakers) who are Jewish and somewhat liberal, so one must be careful of their bias.

WORD STUDIES

Vine's Expository Dictionary of Old and New Testament Words

This is a one-volume reference guide for both Hebrew and Greek words. No knowledge of Greek or Hebrew is required. It sometimes makes too much out of roots and component parts of words but is still helpful.

New International Dictionary of New Testament Theology

This is a three-volume work of detailed study. Knowledge of Greek is not essential.

Theological Wordbook of the Old Testament

This is a two-volume resource keyed to *Strong's Concordance*. You must have *Strong's* or know Hebrew to use this.

DEVOTIONAL AND SPIRITUAL LIFE

These resources provide a wealth of material, old and new, designed to encourage spiritual living.

Time to Get Serious by Tony Evans

Balancing the Christian Life by Charles Ryrie

The Pursuit of God by A. W. Tozer

Knowing God by J. I. Packer

Loving God by Charles Colson

The Kingdom Agenda Devotional by Tony Evans

CHRISTIAN MAGAZINES

These provide a means of keeping abreast of contemporary issues from an evangelical perspective.

Christianity Today

Leadership Journal

Moody Monthly

Discipleship Journal

Eternity

Grace in Focus

ELECTRONIC RESOURCES

Blue Letter Bible

Logos Bible Software

APPENDIX B

———————————— ◆ ————————————

MINISTRY OVERVIEW

The Urban Alternative (TUA) equips, empowers, and unites Christians to impact *individuals, families, churches,* and *communities* through a thoroughly kingdom agenda worldview. In teaching truth, we seek to transform lives.

The core cause of the problems we face in our personal lives, homes, churches, and societies is a spiritual one; therefore, the only way to address it is spiritually. We've tried a political, social, economic, and even a religious agenda.

It's time for a **Kingdom agenda**.

The Kingdom agenda can be defined as the visible manifestation of the comprehensive rule of God over every area of life. The unifying central theme throughout the Bible is the glory of God and the advancement of His kingdom. The conjoining thread from Genesis to Revelation—from beginning to end—is focused on one thing: God's glory through advancing God's kingdom.

When you do not have that theme, the Bible becomes disconnected stories that are great for inspiration but seem to be unrelated in purpose and direction. The Bible exists to share God's movement in history toward the establishment and expansion of His kingdom highlighting the connectivity throughout which is the kingdom. Understanding that increases the relevancy of this several-thousand-year-old manuscript to your day-to-day living, because the kingdom is not only then, it is now.

The absence of the kingdom's influence in our personal and family lives, churches, and communities has led to a deterioration in our world of immense proportions:

- People live segmented, compartmentalized lives because they lack God's kingdom worldview.
- Families disintegrate because they exist for their own satisfaction rather than for the kingdom.
- Churches are limited in the scope of their impact because they fail to comprehend that the goal of the church is not the church itself, but the kingdom.
- Communities have nowhere to turn to find real

solutions for real people who have real problems because the church has become divided, ingrown, and unable to transform the cultural landscape in any relevant way.

The kingdom agenda offers us a way to see and live life with a solid hope by optimizing the solutions of heaven. When God—and His rule—is no longer the final and authoritative standard under which all else falls, order and hope leaves with Him. But the reverse of that is true as well: as long as you have God, you have hope. If God is still in the picture, and as long as His agenda is still on the table, it's not over.

Even if relationships collapse, God will sustain you. Even if finances dwindle, God will keep you. Even if dreams die, God will revive you. As long as God—and His rule—is still the overarching rule in your life, family, church, and community, there is always hope.

Our world needs the King's agenda. Our churches need the King's agenda. Our families need the King's agenda. In many major cities, there is a loop that drivers can take when they want to get somewhere on the other side of the city, but don't necessarily want to head straight through downtown. This loop will take you close enough to the city so that you can

THE WONDER OF THE WORD

see its towering buildings and skyline, but not close enough to actually experience it.

This is precisely what we, as a culture, have done with God. We have put Him on the "loop" of our personal, family, church, and community lives. He's close enough to be at hand should we need Him in an emergency, but far enough away that He can't be the center of who we are.

We want God on the "loop," not the King of the Bible who comes downtown into the very heart of our ways. Leaving God on the "loop" brings about dire consequences as we have seen in our own lives and with others. But when we make God and His rule the centerpiece of all we think, do or say, it is then that we will experience Him in the way He longs to be experienced by us.

He wants us to be kingdom people with kingdom minds set on fulfilling His kingdom's purposes. He wants us to pray, as Jesus did, "Not my will, but Thy will be done." Because His is the kingdom, the power, and the glory.

There is only one God, and we are not Him. As King and Creator, God calls the shots. It is only when we align ourselves underneath His comprehensive hand that we will access His full power and authority in all spheres of life: personal, familial, church, and community.

As we learn how to govern ourselves under God, we then transform the institutions of family, church, and society from a biblically based kingdom worldview.

Under Him, we touch heaven and change earth.

To achieve our goal, we use a variety of strategies, approaches, and resources for reaching and equipping as many people as possible.

BROADCAST MEDIA

Millions of individuals experience *The Alternative with Dr. Tony Evans* through the daily radio broadcast playing on nearly **1,200 radio outlets** and in over **130 countries**. The broadcast can also be seen on several television networks and is viewable online at TonyEvans.org. You can also listen or view the daily broadcast by downloading the Tony Evans app for free in the App store. Over 4,000,000 message downloads occur each year.

LEADERSHIP TRAINING

The Tony Evans Training Center (TETC) facilitates educational programming that embodies the ministry philosophy of Dr. Tony Evans as expressed through the kingdom agenda. The training courses focus on leadership development and discipleship in the following five tracks:

- Bible & Theology
- Personal Growth
- Family and Relationships
- Church Health and Leadership Development
- Society and Community Impact Strategies

The TETC program includes courses for both local and online students. Furthermore, TETC programming includes course work for non-student attendees. Pastors, Christian leaders, and Christian laity, both local and at a distance, can seek out The Kingdom Agenda Certificate for personal, spiritual, and professional development. Some courses are valued for CEU credit as well as viable in transferring for college credit with our partner school(s).

The Kingdom Agenda Pastors (KAP) provides a *viable network* for *like-minded pastors* who embrace the Kingdom Agenda philosophy. Pastors have the opportunity to go deeper with Dr. Tony Evans as they are given greater biblical knowledge, practical applications, and resources to impact individuals, families, churches, and communities. KAP welcomes *senior and associate pastors* of all churches. KAP also offers an annual Summit held each year in Dallas with intensive seminars, workshops, and resources.

Pastors' Wives Ministry, founded by Dr. Lois Evans, provides *counsel, encouragement,* and *spiritual resources* for pastors' wives as they serve with their husbands in the ministry. A primary focus of the ministry is the KAP Summit that offers senior pastors' wives a safe place to *reflect, renew,* and *relax* along with training in personal development, spiritual growth, and care for their emotional and physical well-being.

COMMUNITY IMPACT

National Church Adopt-A-School Initiative (NCAASI) prepares churches across the country to impact communities by using *public schools as the primary vehicle for effecting positive social change* in urban youth and families. Leaders of churches, school districts, faith-based organizations, and other nonprofit organizations are equipped with the knowledge and tools to *forge partnerships* and build *strong social service delivery systems.* This training is based on the comprehensive church-based community impact strategy conducted by Oak Cliff Bible Fellowship. It addresses such areas as economic development, education, housing, health revitalization, family renewal, and racial reconciliation. We assist churches in tailoring the model to meet specific needs of their communities while simultaneously addressing the spiritual and moral frame of reference. Training events are held annually in the Dallas area at Oak Cliff Bible Fellowship.

Athlete's Impact (AI) exists as an outreach both into and through the sports arena. Coaches are the most influential factor in young people's lives, even ahead of their parents. With the growing rise of fatherlessness in our culture, more young people are looking to their coaches for guidance, character development, practical needs, and hope. After coaches, athletes are next on the influencer scale. Athletes (whether professional or amateur) influence younger athletes and kids within their spheres of impact. Knowing this, we have made it our aim to equip and train coaches and athletes on how to live out and utilize their God-given roles for the benefit of the kingdom. We aim to do this through our iCoach App, weCoach Football Conference, as well as resources such as *The Playbook: A Life Strategy Guide for Athletes.*

RESOURCE DEVELOPMENT

We are fostering lifelong learning partnerships with the people we serve by providing a variety of published materials. Dr. Evans has published more than 100 unique titles based on over 40 years of preaching, whether that is in booklet, book, or Bible study format. The goal is to strengthen individuals in their walk with God and service to others.

For more information and a complimentary copy of
Dr. Evans' devotional newsletter, call (800) 800-3222
or write TUA at P.O. Box 4000, Dallas TX 75208,
or visit us online at www.TonyEvans.org

ACKNOWLEDGMENTS

———— ♦ ————

I am extremely grateful to the Moody Publishers family for their partnership with me in the development of this series of books for pastors and ministry leaders. Special thanks go to Greg Thornton who has been with me on this publishing journey with Moody Publishers from the start. I also want to thank Heather Hair for her collaboration on this manuscript. I want to acknowledge the Tony Evans Training Center, under the leadership of John Fortner, for the use of some course material which appears in this book. No book comes to life without editorial assistance, and so my thanks also includes Kevin Emmert, Michelle Sincock, and Duane Sherman.

Life is busy,

but Bible study is still possible.

tonyevanstraining.org

Explore the kingdom. Anytime, anywhere.

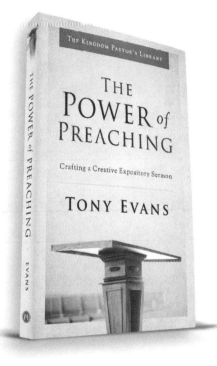

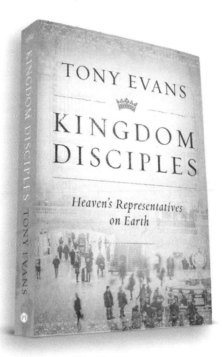

YOU'RE AT WAR.
ARE YOU WINNING?

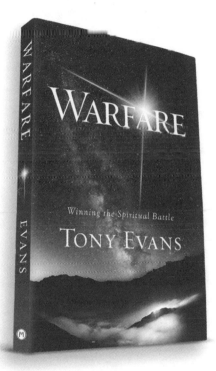

Warfare is a guide to seeing and fighting the most important battles. In it, you'll learn to identify spiritual warfare, how to use the arsenal of spiritual weapons God provides, and how to claim the victory God already won. When we fight the right battles with the right weapons, we win.

978-0-8024-1817-3 | also available as an eBook